INTO THE DAYLIGHT:
A WHOLISTIC APPROACH TO HEALING

This book is an account of the personal and collective struggles of First Nations people and how the principles which held traditional societies together can be used to promote harmonious and cooperative relationships by both aboriginals and non-aboriginals. Calvin Morrisseau outlines in it the fundamentals for healing that he has learned over twenty years through his training in counselling and addiction studies; his education in traditional practices by aboriginal elders, healers, and teachers; and his personal recovery from alcoholism, drug addiction, abuse, and the effects of assimilation, racism, and poverty.

The model of healing Morrisseau advocates is simple, insightful, and based on the values that allowed aboriginal people to live in accord with each other in the past. His approach centres on people accepting responsibility and making choices that give them the freedom required to enter into recovery by recapturing their sense of harmony, cooperation, sharing, balance, and spirituality. The deepest healing takes place on a spiritual level. Morrisseau describes an interdependent system of individuals, families, and communities in which needs, desires, values, and purpose are communicated, and the responsibility to ensure everyone has an opportunity to grow to their full potential is shared. The book is unique in that it offers guidance on ways in which communities can heal.

While the book was written for those who work with aboriginal people, the wholistic approach Morrisseau uses can benefit anyone. The healing model can be used by an individual seeking to heal himself, by a professional as a tool for assessment and treatment, and by a community in crisis.

CALVIN MORRISSEAU is Program Manager at the Wee-chi-it-te-win Child and Family Services in Fort Frances, Ontario.

CALVIN MORRISSEAU

Into the Daylight: A Wholistic Approach to Healing

UNIVERSITY OF TORONTO PRESS
Toronto Buffalo London

Reprinted 1999

ISBN 0-8020-4341-0 (cloth)
ISBN 0-8020-8162-2 (paper)

Printed on acid-free paper

Canadian Cataloguing in Publication Data

Morrisseau, Calvin
  Into the daylight : a wholistic approach to healing

  ISBN 0-8020-4341-0 (bound)   ISBN 0-8020-8162-2 (pbk.)

  1. Indians of North America – Canada – Medicine   2. Healing.
  I. Title.

  E78.C2M675 1998   362.1'089'97071   C98-930475-2

University of Toronto Press acknowledges the financial assistance to
its publishing program of the Canada Council for the Arts and the
Ontario Arts Council.

This book is dedicated to the women in my life: my mother, Cecile, whose courage and commitment to sobriety showed me that the smallest light shines brightly in the dark, my wife, Mona-Rose, whose unending belief in me gave me the courage to believe in myself, and finally, my daughter, Nakita-Rose, whose innocent faith in me allowed me to enter into the daylight with the poise and dignity of a warrior.

Contents

Acknowledgments

There have been so many people who have helped me in this venture. First is my lovely wife, Mona-Rose, who supported and encouraged me. Her kind and gentle suggestions encouraged me to finish what I had started and helped me to believe what I wrote was important enough for others to read.

I want to thank my daughter, Nakita-Rose, for teaching me about little girls and what is important in father-daughter relationships. She taught me to love and respect her so that one day she will grow up to love a man who loves and respects her. My other children, Jason, Daniel, and Calvin Jr, taught me that no matter what, there is always hope.

I wish to acknowledge and thank Zorica Benkovic for sorting and reading through the manuscript many times in the past year and for her kind suggestions. Only with kindness and respect is entering into the daylight possible.

I wish to thank all my many friends in Whitefish Lake First Nation who put up with me during those final days when I was afraid I would not succeed.

I wish also to thank my father, Albert. Although he may not have realized it, the day he stopped drinking he gave me hope for the future. For that I can never be grateful enough. Finally I thank my mother, Cecile, who passed to the spirit world before this manuscript could be published. Her blessing of this work gave me the motivation to finish.

Calvin Morrisseau
November 1997

INTO THE DAYLIGHT:
A WHOLISTIC APPROACH TO HEALING

Introduction

I was born in Fort Frances, Ontario, and raised on Couchiching First Nation, a community of approximately 500 reserve residents. Over the years, partly due to increased technology and the result of Bill C-31, many people and many 'things' have changed. Growing up, I don't remember going to restaurants, eating fresh fruit, attending movies, using laundromats, or having running water, indoor toilets, freezers, electric stoves, or paved driveways. I do remember the poverty, the drunkenness, community apathy, and a great need for family secrecy and denial.

I remember family and friends having to threaten the town of Fort Frances with a blockade to get water flowing into the community. In my culture, water is considered to be the foundation of life, but we at a young age had to labour hard to enjoy a cool drink or a warm bath. What most children thought of as normal, we considered a luxury. Having the town refuse to install a few miles of pipe to bring water into our community signified to me (and many others, I'm sure) just how insignificant and powerless we 'Indians' were – a group that was once a proud and self-reliant people.

At one time, the land our ancestors lived on was able to sustain the people. We did not need to rely on others to provide the necessities of life. There was a relationship based on respect between the Anishinabe and who we call Mother Earth. Nothing would take place in life without first considering our mother, the

Earth, and it was this relationship to our mother which laid the foundation for all other relationships we would pursue through life.

Prior to our discovery of Columbus, no one person was more important than the next. All members needed each other's cooperation to survive in a harsh and unforgiving environment. This harsh environment also helped its people by bringing them closer together in a cohesive and interdependent family unit. Everyone within the community was held sacred. The philosophy of sharing was instilled in children from the time they were old enough to understand. Respect for all of creation was taught as a discipline which guaranteed harmony among its members. This harmony in turn guaranteed cooperation among members and became a value expressed in their spirituality. The circle of life fully encompassed all of the Creator's children. It included four elements: humans, animals, plants, and minerals. Each of these beings were considered brothers and sisters to one another, thus deserving of respect and honour. Not respecting all of creation would result in having the offender bring great shame on himself, his family, and his community.

At this time, all things contained within themselves a spirit. That spirit was our connection to the Creator, whose voice we heard through Mother Earth. The world of the spirit would come amongst us either through a quiet stream, the sight of a hawk during times of disturbance, or the glory of a rising sun. There was, and is, no difference between the world of the spirit and the physical world.

For this reason, our ancestors are just as important and real to us today as they were when they physically walked the earth. It is not surprising for us to see our relatives and loved ones in our visions and dreams. These dreams often tie us to the world of the spirits and thereby create a foundation embedded both within the physical and the spiritual world.

Historically, our people have been caretakers. For our ancestors, putting aside one's own needs for the sake of the family and community was necessary to maintain harmony and cooperation. This kind of sacrifice became a vital part of our value system. We were rewarded for that undying loyalty and reprimanded through shame and guilt whenever we allowed our own needs to take precedence over the family's needs. As individual family members, we were considered to be an interdependent part of the group. This form of cooperation was based on a mutual respect for one another, thereby fostering sharing as a way of expressing that esteem.

The ethic of noninterference allowed members of society to experience life in each their own way, thus creating a reality based upon their own experience. Living cooperatively meant ensuring that all members of society had a responsibility in terms of child care and meeting basic human needs. Everyone was expected to provide food for those who had none and warmth for those who were cold. By providing food and warmth, both trust and love were demonstrated to all members of the community. This love transposed into a sense of self-worth and a feeling that we all were brought into this world complete and belonging. This feeling of completeness gave us our identity and the ability to identify with our community, our families, and our own life experience.

We have moved away from thinking that *all* is equal and sacred to a way of thinking based upon power and control. Having assimilated into a system based upon the concepts of a hierarchy, where those who have the power are found at the 'top,' we have in turn moved away from the concept that everything in life is connected and have developed a reliance on the idea that individuality is what is important. This has brought about changes in the way our communities interact with one another, and has wrought profound effects on our personal relationships, where the roles of the community, the extended family, and the individual have become devalued and disconnected.

No longer do we see or act as if our elders were important to our society. Instead, we see them as burdensome to our new-found lifestyle, one based on an earning of self-worth through the possession of material things, particularly those material 'things' the dominant society so relishes.

In my view, modern psychiatry and medicine have done their

damage to Anishinabe people by suggesting that wholistic healing is not a *natural* way of dealing with our problems. Mainstream society tells us you must have a PhD or equivalent
certificate to heal others. This concept is not only invalid for our
people – it does not consider the importance of our elders and
traditional healing methods – but damaging, because mainstream healers do not always understand us. Native healing is
done on the intrinsic level: healing is a matter of the heart and
not just the 'head.' I suggest that deep inside all of us lies a gentle pearl which gives us all the ability to be healers. What we lack
is the confidence and knowledge to recognize what is important
in healing. It is this gentle pearl that must be cultivated and
brought back to life.

For years I (like many of my people) knew nothing of our history, creation story, beliefs, values, customs, and traditions. I
knew only that Indians were savages 'inferior' to the non-native.
As our culture began to change, our whole system of sharing and
interdependency slowly began to shift towards an individualistic
perception of life. This shift, in turn, destroyed the sacred ties
that connected our families and communities with one another.
As a result, I believe many Anishinabe people are people who are
in pain. This painful cycle appears to take the form where the
individual, their family, and their community become alienated
from each other's existence.

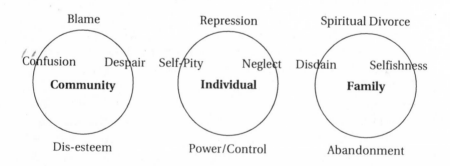

FIGURE 1

This book is about accepting responsibility and making choices that give us the freedom to enter into recovery and recapture the *cooperation, sharing, balance,* and *spirituality* that enabled our ancestors to live in harmony with each other and Mother Earth.

I am not suggesting that I know everything about traditional healing methods. Instead, I plan to offer different ways of viewing healing that challenge mainstream society. What I hope to do is provide you with some paradigms of not only how to work with Anishinabe people, but how we can use these concepts to bring healing to our brothers, sisters, families, and communities.

The model of healing I propose was developed from over twenty years of recovery from alcohol and drug addiction. As I continued to recover slowly from my own addictions, I began to realize that I could not heal completely unless I developed a sense of who I was in relation to my family and community. I realized I was more than an individual. In spite of my resistance, the teaching of my family and community was a part of me.

The concepts in this book are universal and can be integrated into any part of life to build better relationships at home, work, school, or community. For those who uphold ideas of equality, these concepts will integrate easily into your already existing repertoire of skills, but for those lives patterned by patriarchal power, the lessons will call for a complete reanalysis and realignment of values within your own experience. That is, if you can ...

1

The Individual

Today our young people are going off to school, and often when they return they have to be re-educated. I can best illustrate this through an example:

A young man returned to his community after attending college for a number of years. He was asked by the elders to address the community on what he had learned and to thank them for the opportunity of his education. As he talked he referred to all the things he had learned and often spoke of 'I' or 'me.'

The elders sitting in the group listened patiently while the young man spoke. After a short period of time, one of the elders stood up, cutting the young man off, and spoke to both him and the community. The elder stated that he had listened to the young man and began to reprove him for using the words 'I' and 'me.' He said, 'We have sat here and listened carefully to what you were saying. We are discouraged by your words. We have heard you say the word "I" at least ten times. Do you not remember that those words separate yourself from the rest of us? Do you not realize that in our language, in our belief, we are all together? There is no room for "I" because we are all family. We are all relatives depending upon each other for support and love. My child, each time you say I, you make us feel as if you no longer need us, that somehow your education can replace all the Creator has given us to guide our lives.

'We are afraid for you. We are worried that you will now feel

superior to us because we do not have this education. Your words tell us you may have forgotten some important things you learned from us, your teachers. Our Creator created us as one family, your first family, which includes all of creation, to which we are all connected through our families and our communities. None among us has had to stand alone. We were not superior, nor did we pursue our own interests. We always cared for each other, sometimes by putting others needs before our own and only doing what was best for everyone.

'My son, do you not remember these things? Do you not remember when your father was sick and could not work to get food? Do you remember how we all got together and ensured you had a full stomach and a warm house? We do this because we depend on each other. It is our responsibility to care for each other. This "I" of which you speak reminds me of greed. It reminds us to be careful not to be greedy and to share what we have. When other men are always asking for things, we ask to be able to give things. Our ceremonies speak to this. When a child receives a name, the parents have a giveaway. In our way, it is the giving which beseeches the honour. It is the receiving which makes us humble.'

'So tractable, so peaceful, are these people,' Columbus wrote to the king and queen of Spain, 'that I swear to your Majesties there is not in the world a better nation. They love their neighbours as themselves, and their discourse is ever sweet and gentle and accompanied with a smile; and though it is true that they are naked, yet their manners are decorous and praiseworthy' (Dee Brown, *Bury My Heart at Wounded Knee*, p. 1).

Although Columbus was gravely mistaken when he gave the name Indies to the Anishinabe, what he really describes to the king and queen of Spain was a society in which people respected each other. Everyone was important, equal, and held sacred. Wholistic is the word used by Anishinabe to describe the egalitarian view of the human experience. As an individual within a community, everyone had a responsibility to ensure that they fulfilled certain roles in society.

The circle in Figure 2 illustrates what our responsibilities were:

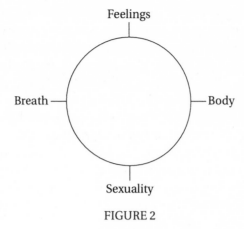

FIGURE 2

Our responsibility to our feelings, body, sexuality, and breath had an important purpose. If each individual carried a spiritual and balanced sense of *who* they were, *where* they belonged, and *what* they were required to do (for themselves), each would as a result experience a sense of purpose. By ensuring that we maintain a sense of *balance* instead of *control* over our feelings, body, sexuality, and breath, we in turn demonstrate to our Creator that we respect what is considered to be 'on loan' to us during our stay here on Earth. For this reason, in native society the answer to the question of who we are not only lies within the confines of our families and our communities but also within *ourselves* and our *spirits*.

Our Responsibility to Our Feelings

Brad's Story:

I remember every time I heard a sharp click, like that of a portable tape machine clicking off, I would feel a shiver of fear go through my entire body. I never could understand why that happened until one day my sister revealed that my father had put a gun to my head and pulled the trigger. All of a sudden, the memory of that experience came flooding back to me, and through therapy I was able to see that my body had never forgotten the experience.

I saw myself as the twelve-year-old boy shivering at the drunken sight of his father. I remembered my father laughing and picking me up by the collar and saying, 'I'm the toughest.' I also remembered the fear I would experience when my father went to the other room and pulled my two brothers out of bed, lining all three boys up against the wall. My father then took his rifle and cocked it into a firing position, put the gun to my head, and pulled the trigger. As a young boy, I heard the sound of metal on metal and I wasn't sure if I was even alive. I heard my father laugh and turn to his drunken buddies for approval. He then turned to me and said to go to bed. Throughout that experience, I don't remember crying or wetting my pants. In the morning, no one spoke about the incident.

Within larger native society, an individual was responsible for ensuring he maintained his own sense of balance by being responsible for his own feelings. For many years, our people conditioned themselves to believe that our feelings were not important. From the time we were taken from our families and placed in residential schools, we began to learn to repress the Creator-given feelings we had for our families, communities, and our way of life. Repression of our feelings and repression of our ceremonies, vehicles to help us deal with our feelings when we attempted to assimilate with non-native culture, created in us a sickness which went deep into our hearts. Many of our people turned to alcohol and drugs to deal with this dissonance.

With the use of alcohol and drugs came other tragedies. We lost our ability to parent. We lost our ability to communicate with our children. Alcohol, drugs, and family violence contributed to a deep and deliberating sense of shame. No longer were we teaching our children to do those things that were honourable. Instead, through the power of example, we taught our children to cope with life using addictive substances, power, and control. Our feelings became muddled in worthlessness and self-pity. We became ashamed of ourselves and tried desperately to hide those feelings from others.

Because we didn't like ourselves, we began to shift the responsibility for our feelings onto others. Blame became an important part of our vocabulary. We blamed our parents, our communities, and the fact that we were 'Indians' for the ever increasing loss of control over our own lives. The more we lost control, the more we needed to exert control. With those in authority too powerful or too far away for us to exert any measure of restitution, we inflicted revenge upon our elders, women, and children. Family violence became an issue passing from generation to generation. Addictions and family violence became twin sisters controlling many who fell prey to their power and deception.

That kernel of change, the false sense of power afforded through addiction and violence, would become our undoing. The hallmark of those sisters would become our inability to accept, process, and validate our feelings. Thus our ability to deal effectively with our feeling would become a key point in any type of recovery. We had to deal with the fear and vulnerability expression of feeling brings.

In her book *Changing Course*, Claudia Black describes what she calls fear of feelings in this way: 'You may have a lot of fear regarding the consequences of showing your feelings, possibly as a result of what happened when you were a child. If you showed your dad you were angry, you were apt to be hit across the face or told you didn't have anything to be angry about. If you showed you were sad, nobody was there to comfort you, to validate that sadness. Maybe you were told to shut up or you were really going to get something to cry about.'

The dominant culture has given aboriginal people the message that they should remain quiet. In its policy of assimilation and condemnation of aboriginal religion and custom – in which our elders and healers were banned from traditional methods of healing – we have been, in essence, told to 'shut up.' The implication that our religion and culture was worthless has created a feeling of shame for our beliefs.

If we could no longer use traditional means of expressing our gratitude and grief, it became logical that denial would become central to aboriginal people. Common knowledge tells us that we cannot live for long without expressing those feelings; eventually they will surface in our behaviour.

Abuse became another means of expression. Fighting amongst

ourselves became a way of life. As we began to abuse our elders, women, and children, we convinced ourselves that the victim was the one responsible for it. The cycle of violence continued from one generation to the next, passed down from father to son, mother to daughter, in an unchecked spiral which would destroy our children. Instead of passing down the teachings of our people, we passed down the noxious effects of trying to become people we were not. The denial of our responsibility for our own feelings by blaming others became the first step in our own self-destruction. Losing touch with our feelings, we became unable to teach our children how to properly deal with them.

When we enter into recovery, we must, then, consider whether we accept responsibility for our feeling or whether we still tend to blame others for them. Our children model our behaviour. If we say, 'You make me mad' instead of 'I am angry,' it is likely our children will follow and use language which demonstrate blame instead of acceptance of responsibility.

In reality no one can make you angry. Anger is our reaction to an event, thought, or action, and therefore we must own our feelings if we are going to be able to express them in a manner which does not intentionally hurt another. We can teach our children through example and modelling that feelings are normal and gifts given to us by the Creator. They should neither be feared and controlled nor be allowed to control us.

In teaching our children, we must draw on the distinction between our feelings and our behaviour. We must show our children through example that it is admissable to be angry, and that there are appropriate ways of expressing that anger. While dealing with my own sexual abuse, I went into the bush, and at the top of a hill I screamed at the top of my lungs, yelling at the Creator, my parents, my abuser, and the world for the injustice done to me. This discharge released years of pent-up emotions. I needed to tell someone exactly how I felt. I could not deny my feelings simply because someone else might not approve. When someone does something which hurts or angers me, it is my responsibility to express those feelings.

In the Anishinabe way, within the sacred sweat lodge in the

presence of the grandfathers I was able to express my feelings in the darkness of our mother's womb. I also wrote many letters to my inner child, my parents, and my abuser. Following the expression of my anger, I was able to deal with the deeper issue of hurt, fear, shame, and guilt surrounding my abuse. I learned through this process that forgiving my abuser was not necessary to healing, but I believe it enabled me to take responsibility for my feelings. It allowed me to move beyond the anger and pain and come to conclusion about the abuse.

I have been told by many elders that there are four things you can do with our pain.

1. You can run away from it.
2. You can become numb repressing the memory, or deny it.
3. You can fight it, wage war against yourself, your family, or society.
4. Or you can deal with it, learn from it, help other who experience similar traumas, thereby making it your friend.

FIGURE 3

Whenever I conduct workshops on alcoholism or family violence, I often remark that our lives are determined by the choices we make. When I came to terms with my alcoholism, I knew I could no longer run from it. I could no longer fight it because the alcohol had me beat. There was simply no fight left in me. I knew deep inside myself that alcohol was truly a power greater than me because it was the alcohol which governed my life.

I came to a point where I was running out of choices. I could continue to drink and die as a result of suicide, or I could go through a kind of mental collapse. After treatment I began to attend self-help meetings and share feelings I never thought possible to experience. People began to respect me and I began to respect myself. I saw that everything that had happened to me, although traumatic and sometimes shameful, could actually be turned into something positive. I began to see that my experience could benefit others if I did not hide those experiences from others.

Our Responsibility to Our Body

One day I attended a workshop on sexual abuse. In it the presenter talked about the characteristics of sexual abuse. One of those characteristics was cutting or carving – the victims' way of asking for help by cutting themselves with knives or razor blades.

I found this to be interesting since in our culture the body is an extension of the Creator. It is the Creator's vessel, which is only on loan to us. It also reminded me of a time when I was eighteen years old. At that time, I was not taking responsibility for my actions, thoughts, or feelings. I blamed my parents for all the problems I was having. I was drinking heavily and drug-dependent. I came home from a party drunk and got into an argument with my parents because they confronted me about my drinking. My parents were sober at the time and beginning their journey to healing using a self-help program.

I yelled at them, claiming everything was their fault. I took a fillet knife and slashed my forearm. I was rushed to hospital, only to be released the next day. Two weeks later, I did exactly the same thing. I did not understand that whenever I did something which hurt me, I inflicted the same wound on those who loved me. In my self-centredness, I thought the only one I was hurting was myself. Little did I know my mother often cried herself to sleep, begging God to help me.

We are responsible to take care of this body. Our body is important in a spiritual sense because it is the vessel which houses the spirit. Our body was given to us for our use by the Creator. We do not own it, nor can we do whatever we want with it. Any actions towards our bodies and others' should always be taken with respect. Our bodies are the vehicles which mobilize our actions, and our actions are more important than our words. Our words have the power to destroy or heal. Everything we say and do is important in relation to who we are and what we do. It must be recognized that our bodies contain the spirits connecting us with Mother Earth and the Creator.

Many of our elders believe our bodies are 'on loan' to us. Since they are only on loan, we have the responsibility to take care of them. We do this by eating properly and watching what we put into our bodies. When I was young child, our family did not have running water. We had to haul water from Rainy Lake, which was about a mile from our house. I was not diligent in taking baths because when I used water it meant I would have to haul it from the lake. Sometimes I would get so dirty you could see it on my body, especially around my ankles and feet.

One Christmas later in life, I made a joke and said that one day I had decided to wash my feet and discovered a pair of socks that I thought I had lost. When I first said this, everyone in my family laughed, but then there was silence followed by a short period of discomfort. What I had said was true, and the silence indicated to me that there was still hurt left in us from the neglect we had experienced.

I know that our parents did not want to neglect us. However, without running water, it was difficult to take regular baths. As I grew in understanding of alcoholism after my recovery, I learned that my parents were also victims of King Alcohol. They lived in this realm, forgetting the children I believe they loved very dearly. This had more to do with their alcoholism than their ability to parent. Without alcohol, both my parents would have been excellent role models. But most weekends were spent with my parents either away or at home drinking. I never thought of myself as being neglected as living with the effects of alcohol became normal.

Living in a home organized around pain became a normal part of life. I expected my parents to go drinking on weekends. I never thought of myself as a child who was the victim of neglect because I learned very early in life to take care of myself. I think the neglect came from the poverty we experienced and the situation on the reserve. What I mean is without running water it was easy to neglect our bodies. It is easier to go without a bath than to go out and walk a mile with a pail in hand to fetch the water. Getting water was a hard job. It was a luxury to have a full barrel of water, and it meant we had worked hard to get it. It did not matter if it was winter or summer: getting water was a chore.

One winter I can remember my brother pushing the sled which carried a barrel of water on it. He was pushing the sled from behind and water was splashing over the top of the barrel. I was pulling the sled in the front, and when we stopped for a rest, the water that splashed on my brother froze to his face and clothes. I remember laughing because he looked funny with all that ice on him. He was crying from being cold and the tears froze his eyes shut.

After that I really felt sad and sorry for him. I tried to warm him by making him work harder. We finally got home and I was able to get him warm. I think sometimes we have good reasons to neglect our bodies. Sadly, we often continue to neglect our bodies even when we have the ability and resources to take care of them. After I reached adulthood, I continued to neglect my body. I did this by not eating properly, drinking too much, and taking my anger out on myself by cutting my arm with a razor blade. I would go for days without eating and then eat only fast foods and things that were greasy.

Having a troubled or difficult childhood is no reason to continue damaging and destructive behaviour. When we become aware that there is a way out of pain, we become responsible for changing the course of our lives. We should concentrate on those things which help us, instead of those things which numb or help us avoid our pain. Pain is our helper because it tells us something is wrong that we need to attend to. Sometimes taking care of ourselves means changing the way we view ourselves.

For years I believed I would never amount to anything. I believed my body was defective because it was a different colour. By coming to understand my own history, I came to accept my body just as the Creator made it. I believe the first step towards wellness is accepting where we are at this particular time.

From my experience, there appears to be an increase in cancer, heart disease, stomach problems, diabetes, sexually transmitted diseases, alcoholism, eating disorders, sex addictions, and vision problems for Anishinabe. With the coming of European culture came a change in our dietary intake. Combining the use of alcohol and other drugs with a change of lifestyle had consequences. There appeared to be a dynamic downward spiral for those who used these substances in excess. We became out of shape both in an emotional and physical way. We drifted from dependency to dependency. Alcohol, food, drugs, sex all became our means of coping with the dramatic changes our societies were experiencing. Those changes had an impact on our bodies, frequently causing us to hate them and, thus, ourselves.

Traditionally, food represented and was symbolic of our relationship to one another. Food meant life, and the sharing of food meant the sharing of one's life. The concept of sharing was important because it challenged our inherent selfishness. By teaching our children to share, we instil in them a value which expects us to see beyond our own needs.

As Anishinabe people, it is our responsibility to redefine our responsibility to our *feelings, sexuality, breathing, and bodies.* Native people today are unsure of who they are and what their roles in society are. In native society, the answer to the question who are we lies within the confines of our family and community. As a people, our bodies are an important part of the family and community. They are respected and seen as a gift, a gift to be cherished by all members of the family and community.

Our Responsibility to Understand Our Sexuality

Within my own life, there was a time when I believed men and women were different. From watching my parents, I thought females were created to serve the man. My young son once commented to his mother, 'All you do is cook, clean, and make Martinis.' What my son was describing was, in essence, my own confused sense of sexuality. I did not for many years recognize that the Creator had created men and women as equals.

The elders say that we are made up of both male and female characteristics. Sexuality has much to do with being complete, being comfortable with oneself, and feeling at harmony with all of creation. Sexuality includes all of what the Great Spirit has given us. It means that as a people we are not greater, or less, than any other. It means that all creation has a spirit and that our sexuality is reflected in our *relationship* with the rest of creation.

On 30 July 1992, my daughter, Anung-Goose, was born. The Creator sent her to me to teach me. From her I learned a great deal about male/female relationships. I learned that the most important male relationship in her life will be with her father. She will seek a man who will be like me, even if she attempts to find someone different. This means I have a great responsibility to treat her with love and respect. By doing so, it is my hope she will seek someone who will treat her with love and respect.

As a people, we did not believe sexuality meant strictly procreation. Sexuality means more than just the act of sexual intercourse. It also includes social and spiritual intercourse. It means that as Anishinabe we are spiritual beings first and that sex is a spiritual experience to be shared on a level where the Great Spirit was present.

Although the harsh environment our ancestors lived in did dictate that male and female roles within society were to be different, each were still valued equally. We were born into this world with only two gifts. Those gifts are our mother and father. If I as a man choose only to follow the ways of my father, paying little attention to the characteristics of my mother, I will not have balance in my life. Instead, I must try to model both my parents. I must accept my role as protector and nurturer. If I do not, I am contributing to my imbalance and incompleteness because I am not nurturing, or sensitive, or speaking from my heart. I must follow the path of both man and woman. We fail to develop our sexuality in the ways of our ancestors when we adopt and accept a system of living that is based upon power and control instead of one based on equality and appreciation.

One of the factors that hinders the development of our sexuality is sexual abuse. In 1991 I began to work on a project which conducted a needs assessment of various First Nations. At that time, discussion about sexual abuse was absent. Denial and refusal to talk about the issue was strong.

After years of attempts to raise awareness about the issue, by challenging the myths, creating support systems in the communities, and planning ways to address the issue, more and more victims of sexual abuse began to come forward. We came to understand how these types of traumas created a sense of low self-worth, which in turn led to the belief that there was something wrong with our sexuality.

Further impacting on our sexuality is the influence of the dominant culture's religious views. Instead of viewing sexuality wholistically, we began to see sexuality as a mere physical expression. We did not take into account the emotional, mental, and spiritual significance of love-making. We came to believe that the expression of love could only be expressed by 'making love' with the one we held attraction to. We thought making love with someone was a conquest. As men, we sometimes viewed the act of making love as a symbol of our manhood. We forgot about the tenderness that must surround love. We did not see that the act of making love begins long before a couple actually becomes 'one.'

As an aboriginal man, I am told by my teachers, our elders, that the act of making love must be a spiritual experience because you bring into that experience all of you, including your spirit. Your spirit is eternal. It was in existence before your physical body. It remains a part of you and goes with you for that eternity. In this vein, sexuality must go beyond the physical to include everything we do in our interactions with others. The Anishinabe way of life means it is who we *are* that is important, not what we do.

We need to be emotionally ready for such a deep commitment. Being emotionally ready has nothing to do with age, as many of us upon entering recovery are not emotionally mature enough to enter into relationships. We need to understand ourselves before we can grasp how a relationship works.

I was once told that relationships are 50–50 – for relationships to be healthy, both partners have to equally give 50 per cent. In my experience as a counsellor, director of a family violence organization, husband, and father, I have learned that relationships are not always 50–50. Sometimes I have to commit and do more than my 50 per cent. There may be times when I have to give 99 per cent, and sometimes the situation is reversed. The degree of commitment means I must give what I can and only take what I need.

From an aboriginal perspective, this way of viewing sexuality follows our traditional teaching about our relationship to the land and its four inhabitants, man, animals, plants, and minerals. We give all we can, and take only what we need.

Our Responsibility to Our Breath

When I was twelve years old, two very important people died as the result of sniffing gasoline. My three cousins and I were sniffing gas, as we wanted to celebrate Canada's one hundredth birthday just like the other members of the community. We stole five gallons of gas from the old sawmill on the reserve and hid it in an old abandoned car. We considered the old abandoned car our party shack. As it began to get dark, all I remember is seeing a candle sitting on the dash board of the car. I never thought anything about it as I watched the flames of the candle turn into little men. Around 11:00 p.m., I believe my guardian spirit made me get up and go home. I waved 'so long' to my friends, telling them I would see them in the morning.

The next day, I was awakened by my uncle yelling 'Clifford and Calvin are dead.' As I got out of bed, I knew who those two boys were who died, and I felt as if a part of me died that day. I later heard that a friend of mine was walking on the road and had seen the car burning. As he ran to the car, he could hear the cries of the children. He wasn't able to get them out of the car.

Shortly after, the friend who saw the car burning moved away to Alberta. I have only seen him twice since that night. Incredibly, we never talked about what happened. The deaths were listed as accidental, and no one in the community ever mentioned what had happened.

I remember blaming myself for what had happened. The memory of that night haunted me well into my thirties. In some ways, I believed I was responsible for their deaths. I thought if I had said something, they would still be alive. I don't imagine anyone could have realized the significance those deaths had on me in terms of self-blame, guilt, and hatred for myself. I could find no relief for my agony.

By the time I was seventeen, I was on a collision course with disaster. I had started drinking, and every time I was drunk I began to relive that night in 1967. I wondered who had brought in the candle to the old abandoned car. I wondered why I was still alive.

The only other survivor of that night was my other cousin. He committed suicide when I was twenty-four. It tells me we both went through the same thing for years following that night. I guess in some ways the candle we used to light our way became the darkness which would follow us for the rest of our lives.

In my grief and self-blame, I had tried to kill myself dozens of times. My will to survive betrayed me each time, creating a failure in my bid for self-destruction. I became the all-time loser who was too chicken to die. I had no respect for life. My anger, pain, guilt, and shame whispered softly at times and screamed at others that I had no right to life. I could not care for anyone's feelings.

The Great Spirit gave us the responsibility for our own breathing. He gave us our life to respect. I realize today that there were many times I should have died, but I believe the Great Spirit took pity on me and intervened. In order to keep our breath of life in me, I needed a sense of purpose. I believe we all need to feel wanted, accepted, believed, and loved. Without that purpose, we become sick inside.

I see around me many of our people searching for that connection to the world. I had to go back and pray and believe that the Great Spirit had a plan for me. Without that sense of purpose, I am left feeling hopeless, sick, and tired of life.

Growing up believing that my life did not mean a great deal to anyone – including myself – I did not have a great deal of respect for it. I thought that life was a battle, an unending war you could never win. I did not see a great deal of hope for my future, nor did I believe anything good would come of my life. Having never dealt with the experiences of physical, emotional, and sexual abuse, I turned to solvents at the tender age of twelve.

The solvent I chose to use was gasoline. It was readily available. Sniffing gas helped me to escape from the drudgery of everyday reserve life. I could have wonderful fantasies and hallucinations. I even thought that sniffing gasoline was harmless. Even if it wasn't, it seemed well worth any risk. Within no time, I became completely hooked. My friends and I began to live for sniffing. Daily sniffing of gasoline became our practice.

When I sniffed gasoline, I could not respect or appreciate life. I was *breathing* into myself my own destruction. There was no one else who was responsible for my sniffing gas, drinking, or doing drugs. I could blame others, a bad childhood, or the government, but in the end no one forced me to sniff the gasoline, take the drugs, or put the bottle to my lips. I alone was responsible, and I alone would be responsible for my life and my willingness to live it.

The question I faced as a young Anishinabe person was how could I reach out to someone or change the way I was when I felt no one cared? We all need a connection to this world. Without that connection to life, we would feel lonely and isolated. People kill themselves because they feel alone. They feel as if no one is on their side. Our system of family has changed. Increased mobility and nonexistent employment opportunities on our reserves have forced many of our people to search for opportunities and a better life away from our reserve communities. Instead of finding a land of opportunity, we find a land of isolation and disconnection. Even if we chose to stay on our reserve communities, the effects of alcohol and drug abuse, poverty, sexual abuse, family violence, and low self-worth create the same divisions in families as those caused by distance.

One of the saddest things that happens to our people is the loss of a child through suicide or an alcohol-related death. In today's world, these tragedies are reported far too often. Childhood should be a time of vibrance, youthful play, and a quest for laughter. What prompts a young person to take her own life?

There are two central themes evident in youth suicide. They are, first, the young person's deep sense of inadequacy, and second, a loss of connection to this world. Every intentional death of a young person is *unnecessary* and *avoidable*.

Many programs are directed towards young people in an effort to keep them busy, but although these programs are vital and necessary, they do not address the total problem. We all are born with a need to feel important, worthy, and wanted. Growing up in a family organized around alcohol, I grew up believing I was unlovable, insignificant, futureless. Children who grow up in homes where alcohol is the central organizing principal – in other words, where alcohol is the primary focus of the caregivers – are often scapegoats and blamed for the parental alcoholism.

While working with children of alcoholics, I discovered the central theme of all children appeared to be their own belief that they somehow had caused their caregiver to drink or take drugs. Many of these young people believed that if they had behaved better, earned higher grades in school, listened to their parents better, kept their room cleaner, or kept out of trouble, this would be enough to stop their caregiver from drinking. Unfortunately alcoholism and drug addictions are two forces greater than our children and our families. No amount of 'good behaviour' will change a person who suffers from their effect.

If we are ever adequately to address youth suicide, we must look at how we as adults are relating to our young people. It is important to give our young ones a sense of belonging and identity. We have to place more importance on our children than on our addictions. We have to understand that children are always listening to what we are saying. They may not listen to our words, but they will certainly listen to actions.

If we really want our children to remain connected to this world, we have to walk the healing path with them. We have to value them for who they are, not for what they accomplish. We have to give them the message that they are valued, worthy, and loved regardless of what they do. That is not to say we excuse all their behaviour, but we can frame it in this manner: 'I love you but I do not like what you are doing.' In this way, the behaviour is confronted while still leaving the young person with a sense of worth and belonging.

Recognizing the importance of places where aboriginal people can meet and share themselves is paramount if our people are to thrive outside their home community. The positive aspect of our culture is that we have many brothers and sisters who can relate to our feelings and way of life.

Sometimes when I am walking down the street in a large city, I will meet an Anishinabe person. It does not matter if he's from a different tribe. There is always some kind of acknowledgment, even if it's simply a look, smile, or nod of the head. Our family system is in some way universal even though our particular tribal customs may be different. In this sense, we are never alone.

That is the message we have to give our young people. There are people who can understand as long as we can reach out. The Great Spirit will always ensure a hand is there. As people in recovery, we must ensure that someone is there to help those who are still suffering. Recovery does carry a responsibility, a responsibility to be there for others, It is the Anishinabe way.

2
The Family

I remember this one day when I was walking downtown with my white friends. One of my friends said, 'Calvin, aren't those your parents?' As I looked up, I saw my mom and dad staggering down the street, obviously heading to another hotel. A deep feeling of shame swept over me – my immediate reaction was to lie. Before I could stop, I heard myself say, 'Those drunken bums are not my parents.'

Something deep inside of me insisted I had done something very wrong. I felt so ashamed, like I had betrayed the very core of my being. I also believe that with that betrayal, a part of me died that day. Later that day, I listened to an old gentleman describe his life to me. He said, 'A long time ago, our families were the most important part of our life. Now they are not. Instead, we see our old people going into old folks' homes to die and seeing very little of their children. We no longer respect our old people, and that bothers me a great deal. Long ago, our old people were recognized for their wisdom and life experience. Today many of our young people think our old people are in the way – a burden to them. When we lose our respect for our elders and our families, we lose respect for ourselves. I wish to tell all our young people that to ensure our future, your vision must include the future. When you see an "old man" or an "old lady" remember, you are looking at yourself.'

This older gentleman continued on and described for me the importance of our aunties and uncles and how they played an important role in rearing our children. He said, 'When receiving a

*name, every child must have two aunties and two uncles.' These
aunties and uncles will be the people who will help the young
one, in some cases the older one, to walk the Red Road. It will be
their responsibility to guide this person who received the name. It
is an important responsibility, one which requires commitment
and wisdom. No young person can stray far from his beliefs when
his family is consistent, supportive, and loving.*

When I think of my childhood, I remember the times when my
father came home drunk. During those times, he was angry and
bitter and ready to take it out on whoever was the closest. Sometimes that person would be me. He would bring with him other
drunks. I think that is what I hated the most, drunken strangers
all around us. We never knew who some of these people were,
but it was as if they had complete run of the house.

It never occurred to me to challenge the belief that my father
reigned supreme. I thought of the biblical teaching to 'honour thy
father and mother' and I figured I would be banished to hell if I
dared to disrespect my parents, regardless of what they did to us.

Despite the abuse and the drunken parties that would take
place around my brothers and sisters, I felt a great sense of loyalty to my family. I knew whatever happened our family must
under all conditions stick together. According to the teachings in
the Catholic school I attended, my parents deserved respect.
The commandments told us to honour our fathers and mothers.
Failure to do so would result in sinning against God and the
Church. To be a sinner meant shame and damnation. I did not
want to go to hell. I excused my parents for everything and
instead blamed myself.

In my childlike mind, I accepted this belief without reservation. I listened to the church as it condemned me for feeling
angry and hurt. It did not understand that drunks had kept the
children awake all night. Eventually I would realize that I was the
cause of all our problems because I was the child. If I could only
be a better child, my parents wouldn't drink – and everything
would be fine.

I began to see Indian people as drunks and bums. I began to

see myself in that same light, and my community and my nation. And there began my spiral into the abyss of chemicals, alcohol, and rebellious behaviour. I did not feel a sense of family. I felt a sense of isolation and shame. This shame came about as a result of what I did and what my people did. When I saw an Indian drunk on the streets, I was looking at my future. Without pride and hope, I got lost and did not follow the Red Road. Instead, I chose to deny my aboriginal heritage and tried to become something I wasn't – white.

The experience of family for natives is different from mainstream society. Instead of focusing on *roles* within families, native families focus on responsibility. We place value on different things. The best way to show this is through an example.

While attending college in 1985, a young native girl found herself in crisis as she had been told that her mother had been hospitalized for a serious illness and had three children still at home. The girl was faced with the dilemma of going back home to the reservation or staying and continuing her education. She decided to go home to help her family. She was quickly confronted by one of her teachers, who insisted she stay and finish school. The girl did not know what to do, and so she contacted an elder and was told that the Indian way was to return home but that no one would blame or judge her if she decided to stay in school.

She decided to stay in school. However, within a few days, she began to feel guilt. She went to see the school counsellor, who told her that sometimes we have to worry about our life and our future. Staying in school was one way of worrying about our future. With that, she received the answer she had sought. Yet contrary to the counsellor's suggestion, this young girl left school and went to help her parents, acknowledging her own sense of values and feeling of collective responsibility. She later returned to school and completed her education.

Why did this young girl forsake her own dreams and ambitions to return home and help her family through these difficult times? How do native people come to make decisions based on what is best for the family? The answer to this lies in what the family teaches its members. It is the family's responsibility to ensure that its members learn four basic teachings. These responsibilities (as shown in Figure 4) are for communication, eating, intimacy, and respect.

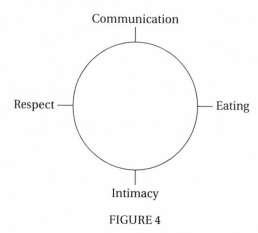

FIGURE 4

The family is responsible for ensuring that children within the family system learn to incorporate these four elements into their life. From the story above, the young girl learned that she had to put aside her own feelings and desires for the betterment of her family. From an aboriginal or traditional perspective, what is described in the above scenario is something that brings honour to the one giving up personal goals for that of their family.

Communication: A Family's Responsibility

One of the losses we experience when we grow up in a home with an alcoholic parent is that of our childhood. This loss of child-hood is reflected in our loss of spontaneity and inquisitiveness. Instead of reacting or acting in reflexive, curious ways, many children who grow up in these homes learn to become invisible. They learn to stay out of the way and keep quiet, never drawing attention to themselves.

*I have always heard that Anishinabe people are stoic. I do not
believe this is entirely true. I do believe that Anishinabe people do
not speak simply for the sake of speaking. We recognize our words
are powerful and so should be used only when necessary. Above
all, our words should be used to reach consensus and should not
be used to divide ourselves.*

*There are many different ways to speak. Our bodies speak
louder than our words. Our bodies have a way of letting others
know when we are telling the truth or when we are lying.*

To learn how to relate to others, we must first learn to how to
communicate. Surviving dysfunctional homes, many of us never
learned how to communicate effectively. Instead, we learned
how to communicate indirectly, expecting others to know what
we wanted without actually asking for it. In my experience, fear
of rejection or being refused something meant I was not worthy
of receiving it. A conversation would usually go like this:

Jill: Hello, Cal. What are you doing?
Cal: Oh, nothing. Why do you ask?
Jill: I was just wondering.
Cal: So what are you doing today?
Jill: I guess I'm going to walk to town (sigh). My leg is so sore,
too. I wish someone could take me.
Cal: (*Feeling angry and manipulated because it has happened
before.*) I'll take you. What time do you want to go?

In the above conversation, the communication was indirect.
Jill did not actually ask Cal to take her to town. She chose to
make Cal feel sorry for her. Also, Cal was not direct and allowed
himself to be manipulated.

In families where alcohol and family violence are present, we
often take responsibility for that which is not our own. In Chapter 1, 'The Individual,' we learned that Cal should be responsible
for his own feelings and his own body. No one can make Cal take
Jill to town. Cal and Jill communicated in a manner that breeds
anger and resentment.

Growing up on my reserve, I learned the arts of verbal and nonverbal communication, but within my family of origin, nonverbal communication played a larger role than verbal communication. Aboriginal people are hunters so it is not surprising that we place a greater importance on this type of interaction.

In our family, we used sign language to communicate. One example of our own variation of sign language is best shown by the following. During our evening meal, my mother would ask for the salt by waving her right index finger and pointing at the object. Everyone in the family came to understand that she was asking for the salt. By watching her, I learned to ask for salt using the same method. When I got married, my wife had to learn this variation of sign language. Now my daughter, Anung-Goose, asks for salt the same way as her grandmother did, and her father.

I have found that speaking only when necessary or speaking nonverbally to others is practised by many of the community people I see as I travel from community to community. Silence becomes a means of communication because who you are is more important than what you do. Let me explain by giving this example.

When I was about ten years old, I was lying on the couch because I did not feel well. My aunt came over to visit with my mother. I did not find this of importance at the time; however, later the significance of this experience stayed with me. My mother was washing the dishes when my aunt arrived. After a short but pleasant exchange of hellos, my aunt sat down and sipped on a cup of tea all the while watching my mom do her daily work. My mom continued with her work.

In total there could have been no more than ten words said between them during her entire visit. Later that day, while we were having supper, my mother told my father that my aunt had come for a visit and that it had been a very good visit. I thought about this. In my mainstream thinking, there has to be verbal dialogue for a visit to be good. Yet for them, I guess the good came about as a result of them just being together instead of having to do or say anything.

When I was working with young chemically dependent adults, I often remembered this visit. As a counsellor, I had to learn to enjoy the silence that sometimes happens in counselling situations. I now see silence as a skill worthy of developing, a valuable tool that can be used to help others and ourselves. Sometimes we can spend too much time talking when we should be listening. Sometimes I will go into my quiet room, burn some sage (a herb used for purification), and just sit in the darkness listening to the silence. Other times I will listen to the birds chirp or the rain fall. Listening is a skill which goes beyond hearing. It involves the five senses because it involves apprehension of nonverbal messages. When we listen to our spouse, friend, coworker, or others, we remain silent until they are done. This little act of respect signifies our respect for them. It is the foundation of good communication.

Sometimes people use silence as a means of controlling a situation. When I was counselling teenage chemical abusers, I remember a young man who came to my office for counselling. It was obvious that he would rather have been anywhere than in my office. Throughout the session, he just sat there staring at me, refusing all my attempts to engage in conversation.

At the end of the session, his mother asked me how the session went. I told her it went very well, which caused a look of surprise on the young man's face. He came back the following week and, just like the previous week, did not say a word. We sat in silence for close to the entire hour before he finally retorted in anger and frustration, 'Are you going to help me or what?' He gave up using silence as a means of control because I would not play his game. We went on to have a very good working relationship.

Without the teaching of my mother and aunt, I would not have recognized the importance of silence. Whenever anyone uses silence as a means of control, I usually respect their wishes to be silent, even when the silence is used in anger. Game playing does not foster good communication because it stops people from knowing who we are and what we are experiencing. This is especially true in relation to the way we are feeling.

Communicating our feelings has to be done in an honest and open way. I remember hearing an elder talk about the need to cry. She said it was important to cry because tears wash the water which washes our souls. Just as our Mother Earth needs rain to clean away the dirt, so do our people need tears to express the pain or joy in our lives. In this sense, tears are seen as signs of strength instead of weakness. Since most communication is done through our actions, what tears are telling everyone is that 'I feel good enough about myself to relate to Mother Earth, to the woman in all of us.'

Since families are responsible for teaching their members about communication, it isn't surprising that many of us never learned how to communicate on a deeper level than words. Feelings are neither right nor wrong. It is usually the way we express our feelings that gets us into trouble.

When I was in my early twenties, I was very impatient. I used my impatience as an excuse to go drinking. I thought everyone made me feel the way I felt. The way I dealt with my feelings was not safe and appropriate. The way I felt became an excuse to use alcohol and drugs.

Before we can express our feelings appropriately, we should find someone we can trust. Sometimes it is difficult to trust others, particularly if we have grown up in a violent or alcoholic home. When I entered into recovery, I told my personal story to anyone who would listen. I even told people about the sexual abuse of my childhood. Eventually someone told someone else. I felt betrayed, yet I learned a valuable lesson: there were those who could not be trusted and there were those who could be trusted. I learned that I needed to have some boundaries around what I should say and when to say it. Today I make a choice in telling my story and I take responsibility for it. I realize that once I tell my story to someone I lose control over it. I learned to be gentle with something as valuable as my own personal journey.

When we enter into recovery, many of us may have to form new families to practise our new communication skills. Healing and talking circles are excellent avenues to practise communicating in an open, honest, and direct manner. It is a safe environment, with no crosstalk and no one to tell you your feelings are wrong. Confidentiality is paramount, and everyone should realize the sacredness of what is being disclosed. Our pain is precious and should be treated as such. To heal, we all need to find a safe place.

Whenever someone tells me their story, I believe they have given me a precious gift. If I can't keep this gift to myself, I have no right to accept it. In a healing, when I hold an eagle feather or a sacred stone, these things are my connections to the spirit world. Therefore, I realize the sacredness of our stories. I believe that is why the Creator gave the responsibility of communication to our families. It is our families who will help us heal through collective responsibility, even if we have to form a new family through a self-help group or a healing circle.

Eating: A Family's Responsibility

I can't say that all my memories of childhood were bad. Whenever my father and mother were sober, they were excellent parents. One of my best memories takes place at our dinner table. My mother was an excellent cook, and it was important to my parents that everyone was home for dinner. In my home, it was difficult for us to express love or concern for each other, but food was seen as a way for my parents to express their love for their children.

When sober, my parents were loving, and even when they went drinking on payday weekends, they always made sure they bought groceries first. I remember waiting for the delivery man to bring the groceries. For us children, it was like Christmas.

Thirty years later, my wife, who is Micmac, told me that in her culture the giving of food to another is a symbol of respect and hospitality. I guess my parents also knew of the importance of food, not only as a means of sustaining life, but of giving life.

The introduction of the refrigerator and freezer did much to change the manner in which native families related to each other. Before the emergence of these appliances, people were required to share their food before it spoiled. With their introduction aboriginal people no longer had to share. Before that, sharing was an important part of the culture. Feasts were seen as an important means of bringing families and communities together.

Not too long ago, I was asked to speak at a conference on aboriginal healing. I talked about food as being an important aspect to healing because the sharing of food meant you were willing to share your life with that person. I remember the day I asked Mona Rose to be my wife. I asked her right after we had enjoyed a romantic meal at a very nice restaurant. I'm not saying she agreed to marry me because I bought her a romantic dinner, but the importance I placed on the atmosphere surrounding the meal meant I was placing importance on our relationship. We can use food to build relationships with others and to sustain our way of sharing with everyone.

Whenever I go to a community and present information on family violence or addictions, the presentation is usually followed by a feast. In our culture, a feast is the appropriate way to follow up on a ceremony, workshop, or meeting. Food to us is more than a substance enabling us to sustain life. Food is *life itself.* To share food with someone is to share life and to honour life itself. The sharing of food builds trust, and trust is significant in the building of healthy relationships. As we begin to heal from our past, it is important to begin trusting.

For those of us who may have been betrayed by our caregivers, trusting others can be one of the largest blocks to recovery. One night at a self-help meeting, I met a young girl who felt guilty because she did not trust everyone in the group. For some reason, this young girl believed trust had to be given freely. She thought trust was the requirement for entry into the self-help meeting. As I watched her grow in the self-help program, I noticed that as she got to know people, she began to disclose things about her life more freely. She began to see that the people in the group needed to earn her trust, just as she needed to feel safe in their presence.

Many believe when we enter into recovery we should blindly trust all those who appear to want to help us. I don't believe this to be a healthy attitude. Trust is something that demands the highest regard. We should not trust everyone. It must be earned and it takes time to trust others. Early in my recovery, I thought I should trust everyone in my twelve-step program. I disclosed some intimate things to a person who was in the program longer than I. Later I found that he had disclosed information about our discussion to another person outside the program. I felt betrayed by him, and in my anger I almost gave up.

Instead of confronting him, I told myself that no one could be trusted. I thought about going out and getting drunk. By not dealing with the problem directly, I had almost reverted to an old coping mechanism – painting everyone with the same brush. This experience instead taught me that there were some people who could be trusted and some who could not, and that it was my job to protect myself. If I decide not to trust someone, I have to realize that trusting is also my choice. I can choose to trust or not to trust. Whichever way I decide, I hold the power of decision.

There are some guidelines I use to determine when and if I should be self-disclosing.

1. I must be disclosing for a specific reason. Self-disclosure should not be a random act but a part of an ongoing relationship.
2. It must concern what is happening at the time, and it should concern the person to whom you are disclosing.
3. It should always be done to help improve a relationship by making the relationship deeper and richer.
4. We should always consider what effect the disclosure will have on the other person.

By bearing in mind these simple guidelines, we can begin a process of trust without leaving ourselves open to hurt. Although trusting is a process that requires risk; we can do so in a way that is respectful of both parties.

Although food and trust are two separate issues, they are connected in aboriginal healing. We as aboriginal people must realize that the use of food to build trust is a universal principle. Mainstream businesspeople have been doing this for generations. What I find intriguing is that we discount the use of food as a therapeutic tool. I think it makes sense to bring the practice of using food into the circle of healing. Celebrating our successes by feasting is one way of honouring our accomplishments.

Food is also a way of showing respect and support to others. When my mother passed into the spirit world, there were many people who brought food over to the family. Although these people did not stay long at my father's house, we recognized their gift of food as their way of expressing compassion and support for us. In this light, food is seen as something much more than a substance to sustain life. Food is life. It represents the sharing of life with others. Even so, we must not let food become the way of sharing. We should couple the sharing of food with the sharing of self.

When we share food with someone, we are really sharing our intimate selves, and so our relationship with food must be one of respect. Food is a gift from the Creator. When we use food to avoid or suppress our feelings, the relationship we have with it can become problematic. I once used alcohol to avoid my feelings; food can be used in much the same way. If we get upset or angry, the best way to deal with it is to talk about it. In this way, we allow our feelings to go through a natural process.

Everyone has feelings that need to be expressed. Anything that interferes in the expressing of those feeling has the potential to hurt us in the long haul. For us to become or remain healthy, we must always respect and share our feelings with someone we can trust. We usually fall into addiction problems when we fail to share innermost selves with someone who can be trusted.

Intimacy: A Family's Responsibility

Early on in my recovery from alcohol and drugs, I met a woman who spoke about allowing someone else to know us on a deeper and more emotional level. I never really understood what she

meant until much later in life. When I met my wife, I was just fin-
ishing four years of counselling for sexual abuse. During that
time, I began to explore ways in which I hid my real self from
other people.

Being an alcoholic and drug-dependent, I quickly learned that
to let people know who I was I needed to trust people enough to
disclose things about myself. In no time, I was telling everyone
what happened to me in childhood. I did not realize I had gone
from being too closed to being too open about things. I had to
learn balance – and that not everyone deserved to hear my story.

As a system, the family is responsible for ensuring that members of the family learn about intimacy. Intimacy can best be described as the degree to which we allow others to get to know us. To form sound relationships around me, I had to learn to find balance between the nurturing and analytical, calculating side of myself. I also had to learn that my trusting was sacred, and that I could choose whom I could trust and whom I could not by listening to that little voice inside of me. I had to learn to trust my own intuition.

My Anishinabe culture teaches me that men are the keepers of the fire and women the keepers of the water. Having too much fire evaporates the water. On the other hand, too much water puts out the fire. All things within the circle of life must operate in balance. So too must our relationships with our partners and our children. Men, in particular, must know and respect the tremendous responsibility they have in teaching our children about intimacy. We must demonstrate through our actions the importance of treating all of God's creations with gentleness and respect. In that way, we will teach our daughters and our sons the importance and sacredness of womanhood. They will see that intimacy means showing affection freely and unconditionally.

The concept of noninterference does not mean we turn a blind eye to injustices like family violence or abuse. What non-interference means is we let the oak tree grow to its potential height. We will protect its right to do so. That is the agreement we have with Mother Earth. Therefore, we must protect our children and women from the ravages of domestic violence and abuse. The end to these tragedies lies not only in the empowerment of women and children, although such a thing serves a valuable purpose. The solution to these tragedies lies also in working with our men, giving them a sense of pride, belonging, and importance. Helping them work through their own abuse by accepting responsibility for their healing is crucial to healing our families.

Recently I talked about family violence and its effect to a group of mainstream family violence workers. I was confronted by one counsellor for using the words 'abuse' and 'healing' in the same breath. He said that men should not be excused for abusing their partners on the basis that they were abused themselves. What he failed to see was that the concept of responsibility allowed us to work with the offender instead of locking him away. Traditionally our families were responsible for teaching about intimacy. In family violence, there can be no intimacy.

For us, the development of intimacy lies in the teaching of those things to our children. As parents and caregivers, we need to teach our young boys to respect women. Our women are the givers of life and deserving of respect. Whenever a man strikes out against a woman, he teaches his children to handle problems with violence. He also teaches his children that it is all right to hit and abuse. From an Anishinabe perspective, striking out against a woman is like striking out against everything we hold sacred, our life, our future, our customs, and beliefs, because our women represent the power which is contained within all these concepts. By weakening women, we are weakening our people.

Respect: A Family's Responsibility

Bless our mothers because after all the things I have done to hurt my mother, she often says, 'At least you always respected us.' I can't say that I agree with her, but I love her for saying it.

I think I was very disrespectful towards my parents. When my

*parents sobered up, I knew I would have to stop blaming them for
all my problems. I don't think I respected anything because I
didn't respect my own life.*

*When my grandfather was still alive, he would often talk to me
about respecting elders. I loved to listen to him tell stories of the
old days and how 'us Indians,' as he use to say, never made a
major decision without consulting the one who had life experience. As I grew to be a man, I forgot these teachings, and I did not
believe respect was important.*

*Whenever I drank alcohol, it created a person I did not want to
be, and yet, I had no control over becoming this person. I lived on
selfishness and greed. I was like a tornado uprooting all of the
relationships in my path. I created a prison and called it love. To
love me meant to give up yourself because I needed you to fill the
great hole in my spirit, and I expected no less.*

Many times we expect or feel we should be respected when we
really have done nothing to deserve or earn that esteem. Our
elders earned this respect because they preserved themselves
over attempts by Christianity and mainstream ideology to
destroy their way of life. They also deserve this respect simply
because they are elders. Within First Nation communities, there
is a great concern expressed about the lack of respect shown
towards our elders. Yet it is not only our elders who are not being
respected – we don't seem to respect ourselves.

Our extended families need to take up their responsibility of
ensuring that our children learn about respect, not only for people, but for all things created by the Great Mystery. I remember
hearing a song performed by a native artist. The song asks the
Creator to make his hands respect all the things he has created.
This respect must be taught to our children from the time they
are old enough to understand. We need to teach them to respect
other people's right to life, the right to make their own decisions,
and the right to allow others to be responsible for themselves.
What respect really means is we allow others the right and
responsibilities to do as they wish with freedom.

Our children, through observation, will judge us by our

actions – not by our words. When we tell our children not to smoke and then light up a cigarette, or tell them not to drink alcohol and then take a glass of beer or wine, they are learning two important lessons. The first lesson is hypocrisy, and the second, that it is fine to do something that is not right; if it were really wrong, parents would not do it. Parents, grandparents, teachers, coaches, and band leaders have to be the *role models* for our children.

I remember as a young teenager seeing many of my people lying on the streets of Kenora, Ontario. I felt deeply ashamed of them and deeply ashamed of myself for feeling the way I did. How could I respect our people when all around me I saw nothing but the dark side of things? I knew from early on in my childhood that my family had always taught me to respect all of life. Yet watching my people lying on the streets passed out from alcohol made it impossible to respect anything, including myself.

If we are truly to become healed, we need to develop and teach our children and grandchildren about respect. Our children will be watching our behaviour to see if we respect others and everything that the Creator has made. Once we learn to respect, we will learn to live in cooperation and harmony with our brothers and sisters.

When we strike out in violence against our children, we are striking out against our future. We are hurting ourselves by weakening the very fabric of our existence by damaging our children's futures. The damage caused by taking our children away through the residential school system and the Children's Aid Society's former policy of abducting children from reserves cut deeply into the future of our people. Instead of nurturing our children, many residential school survivors learned to discipline their children with harsh corporal punishment. As a second-generation residential school survivor and a product of a religious school system, I have had first-hand experience with harsh corporal punishment from both the parental and the school system. We must understand that to heal we need to recognize hitting as a means of disciplining children is wrong.

The Anishinabe way is to teach our children right from wrong by letting them experience the natural consequences arising out of their behaviour. A natural consequence is the natural result of something we do. If I touch a hot stove, the natural consequence is that I burn my finger. I do not need to be punished for it. Our job as caregivers and parents is to teach and guide our children through the natural consequences of our actions in a safe way. We don't protect them from the natural events of childhood; however, we don't make it unsafe for them through neglect and abuse. Our job is to guide our children into adulthood. The Anishinabe parent watches out for things that could harm his children, protects them from those harmful situations while allowing his children to fall, scrape their knee, and get back up.

3
The Community

The old man sat on a hill which overlooked the community of his birth. He remembered a time when the people in the community worked and played together. He remembered that in those days the people valued each other and took responsibility for each other's well being. The children always had an adult they could talk to and ceremonies that gave them a sense of purpose. Now it seems no matter how hard they try, they cannot overcome the social problems which plague his beloved community. The old man bent down and kissed his mother, the earth, and wondered how he could have allowed his people to forget what things in life were important.

He remembered his role as elder, and a tear formed in the corner of his eye. How sad his life had become. He once felt such pride when he thought of the community he came from. He remembered the feasts once held in honour of the changing seasons and how instead of stocking up on wine and beer, his people once stocked up on food to celebrate special occasions. Instead of asking for things, our honour once came from giving things. Today many of the members of his community sought pleasure in material things, instead of those spiritual things they once believed in.

He considered himself a failure, and he began to dread meeting the grandfathers in the spirit world. He could not explain to them how he had failed in his responsibility to lead his people and to educate them on the Anishinabe way of life. Instead what he saw was that many of the people were listening to the death bird, who was disguised as alcohol and selfishness. He saw how the community was being ripped apart by this power far greater than his own. He saw our Mother Earth damaged by strip mining and pollutants in the atmosphere. He wondered how the people drifted so far from what they once believed. Finally he saw all the children crying and forgetting to play their childhood games. Yes, he considered himself a failure and he wept.

Couchiching First Nation is located on the border of the United States. It is a community much like any other First Nation community. During my childhood, many of the community residents suffered from alcoholism, unemployment, drug addiction, family violence, racism, inadequate water and sewer systems, poor housing, and poor health. This is not uncommon among First Nations communities, which have often been referred to as 'Third World countries.' When I was an adolescent, I would often look around my community and dream of the day when I would be able to leave. I believed that by staying in my community I would remain trapped in the same cycle of poverty, violence, and addiction of many of my relatives and neighbours. In a sense, I was my community and my community was me. I once heard someone express it this way, 'When they tear down one of us, they are tearing down all of us.'

Recently I was sitting in a coffee shop and overheard someone say it had been reported the government had sent some Indians children across the country for treatment for solvent abuse. They were disgusted because these children were again using solvents once they had returned from treatment. To them, it was a waste of money; to me, it was a waste of time.

It did not come as a surprise for me to hear that these young people had relapsed. When I first heard of this, I knew immediately the prognosis of abstinence for these young people would at best be poor.

Sending kids to treatment does not consider the *community* in the recovery plan. It does not recognize that the *community* has responsibilities to its members and individuals. The circle in Figure 5 depicts the community's responsibility.

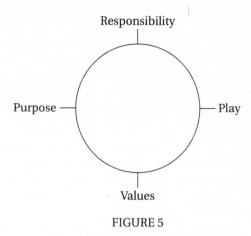

FIGURE 5

The Community's Responsibility for Its Members

In the 1960s, social workers were responsible for taking many of our aboriginal children away and placing them in non-native foster homes. Sometimes these children were placed in foster homes in Europe. I know of a child who was taken away from a sixteen-year-old birth mother and adopted out to a family in Scotland. At the time of the adoption, the child was only one day old. She never knew her birth mother, nor did she know the community from which she came. When she grew up, she had been told of her adoption and that she was an 'Indian' from a place called Ontario.

One day some native leaders were attending a meeting over-seas, and this young lady heard about it. She walked into the meeting and proclaimed that she was Indian like them, and asked if any of them could help her get home. The native leaders assumed responsibility for this lost child and contacted her home reserve. The home reserve, recognizing its responsibility for this lost child, assumed the cost of bringing her home. She was home because the community wanted her home. After more than eighteen years of being lost to the community, she came home to the sounds of drums and celebration. Although the adjustment to her new home was difficult because she had to learn many new things, she did stay on in her new home and community, and lives there to this day.

I speak of *community* as if it were a living entity, and rightly so, for a community has a life of its own. It is made up of many individuals tied together through a collective desire to live in a type of harmony. This harmony must be enforced by a set of rules regulating relationships among its members. These rules are in some sense the laws that governed members of the community. The concept of noninterference is one such community law which shaped relationships among its member by articulating the community's responsibility.

At first glance, noninterference could be interpreted as not interfering in the lives of others. To some degree, this is true. However, through the eyes of those living 500 years ago, noninterference takes on a different meaning. A tree has a right to grow to its full potential, and I, as a creation of the Great Spirit, have the responsibility to ensure it has the opportunity to do so. Hence, I have a right to intervene whenever that right is threatened. All too often, I have heard this concept explain why our brothers and sisters refuse to intervene when they see one of our brothers lying on the street or beating his wife. If we really believed in traditional concepts, we *would* intervene. We would realize that anything disrupting or hurting the group collectively needs to be confronted and dealt with immediately. The harmony of the group is paramount.

Twenty years ago in my community, there was no intervention, no understanding of what responsibility for the members of the community meant. Our chiefs would show up at meetings drunk.

Our elders spoke out against these things, and eventually some of our chiefs began to recover from their drinking problems and began to become positive role models for our young people. We began to see our young people graduating from postsecondary institutions and becoming increasingly confident and cocky when dealing with the federal and provincial governments. We saw our people begin to take a more proactive stance towards the deplorable circumstances surrounding our communities. As communities members, we began to feel more trust and confidence in our leadership, and we began to support them by attending band and community meetings. We began to realize that in order to self-actualize, we needed to take responsibility for ourselves, our families, and our communities. We realized the importance of our communities. We realized that our personal healing had to be in conjunction with the healing of our communities. We realized our communities had a responsibility to its members.

All community members must know and be clear what the vision is for their community. It is the responsibility of our leaders to *ensure a vision*, for without one, we flounder in a sea of apathy and confusion. Our vision must be one of healing for every member of our society.

Play: A Community Responsibility

I was called into a community in order to help it deal with some youths who were damaging band office buildings. As I drove into the community, I noticed the baseball diamond had been neglected and the backstop had deteriorated to a condition that made it impossible to play. I also noticed the children were playing alongside the road.

From my observations, I believed that the community was neglecting its responsibility to provide its members and children with a place to play. Providing children and adults with leisure activities that promote healthy living is a responsibility of the community.

After talking with chief and council, I met with some of the children in the community. From our discussion, I learned of the children's anger and discouragement over the lack of attention given to the children. I also remembered another community that had similar problems but which was able to offset some of the difficulties by giving children and teens some leadership skills through a youth group. This youth group was created to empower the children and teens to have a say in tribal government as well as to give direction to chief and council regarding some of the needs and concerns of our young aboriginal peoples.

In spite of the narrow focus of the group, it wasn't long before some of the group members started planning activities for the community's young people. They went ahead and raised their own funds. Under the supervision of the adults in the community, they raised funds for a new baseball field and other recreational activities. Chief and council recognized that these young people were serious about creating a better atmosphere for young people and created a staff position whose sole responsibility was to liaison between youth and leadership. It was the youth who forced the leadership to assume responsibility for play in this community. For this brief period in time, it was the youth who became the leaders.

I remember the feelings I would experience on Sunday mornings after my parents had been out drinking on the weekend. I felt neglected and unloved during those times. I wished I had a father who would play ball or take me fishing. Although my parents had not physically abandoned me, emotional abandonment can be just as traumatic and can have just as devastating effect. All too often our children act out their boredom and neglect through vandalism and crime.

When this happens, we ask ourselves what is wrong with our children, when really what is happening is, in the circumstances, a natural response.

Children who grow up in alcoholic or violent homes experience a loss of childhood. Many learn to walk before they crawl – and in aboriginal communities, many learn to run before they crawl. This is because in families that are pain-centred oftentimes younger members assume parental responsibility. Instead of enjoying a time when they should be playing, the children are often asked to go through a grieving process instead of learning to imagine and dream.

While conducting a planning process in some First Nations communities, I asked people to dream about all the services they wanted to see in order to end family violence. In some communities, the members couldn't even dream because their initiatives had been refused so many times by the federal government. They were afraid to dream. More important, they were afraid to ask for things, and as a result, many of the children acted our their frustration and apathy, usually on the administration building.

For children who grow up in painful families, feelings of anger, powerlessness, apathy, sadness, anxiety, and disgust are often expressed as a means of getting attention. If Claudia Black, one of the founders of Adult Children of Alcoholics, is correct when she says there are three rules in families where alcoholism is present, those of Don't Talk, Don't Trust, Don't Feel, then it makes sense to assume Canada's aboriginal population – subject to oppression and society's denial of the truth – face even greater hardships in terms of recovery. When one compares the experience of Canada's aboriginals to any other society dominated and forced to accept a different culture, the trauma equates to any people whose whole livelihood has been destroyed. For over 500 years, Anishinabe people have been told to keep quiet, to distrust their own leaders, to abjure their own culture and religion, and to repress anger, frustration, and hurt.

To heal from this tragedy, we must continue to laugh and play. Our laughter can be just as healing as our tears and should never be discounted or thought of as unimportant. It is our great sense of equanimity and humour that will bring us back together as one people – and that includes all aboriginal people. We need to end the labels handed to us by the government of Canada. Our laughter and games will give us an opportunity to come together as one people blessed by the Creator with life. Our children need places to play and they need direction and support in developing appropriate values. By providing our children with activities and equipment, we demonstrate to them that they are important.

When I was in high school, I was a very good miler, meaning I could run a mile very quickly. I remember winning many trophies and bringing them home, yet no one was terribly impressed. In my anger and hurt, I threw them out. I thought I wasn't good enough, that no matter what I did, no one would ever pay attention. I thought that my life and my accomplishments meant nothing. That feeling of not being important, of never being good enough, became the centre of my being. This feeling of inadequacy came out in, 'I'm sorry,' 'I'm stupid,' 'I'm good for nothing,' or 'I'll never amount to anything.'

To find fulfilment, some sense of wholeness, I sought approval later in life from 'misfits,' people I thought who really understood me. It wasn't until these people had completely lost any use of me that even they rejected me that I realized I had graduated to the lowest rung, all the while believing I deserved to be there. It certainly is not the lack of recognition for my many trophies that brought me to this point, but the accumulation of losses and humiliations I experienced.

In simple recognition of the accomplishments of our children, we can help prevent the conditions that flow towards alcoholism and drug abuse. When people feel good about themselves, they don't need substances like alcohol or drugs to make them feel good.

Purpose: A Community Responsibility

The teenage boy lay in his hospital bed wondering how his life had become so mixed up. He thought of the friends he had had since boyhood and wished he could see them once more. Maybe this last meeting could be one in which he could find forgiveness for taking their lives. All he knew today was that he had no reason to go on living, no reason to face another day. He had given up all hope that he would be able to put those things behind him.

As the nurse came into the room, he whispered under his breath for her to go away. He did not want to see anyone, nor did he want to answer any questions. Of course he was a failure, a criminal, a low-life. He needed no one to tell him the truth about what he had become.

The only problem he had was that he felt bad about what he did. He felt remorse about not having a future. His future would be prison or reform school, and this he could not face. So instead he tried to take his own life, only to be found by some kind-hearted soul.

Now he lay in this bed afraid to think of his future, afraid to think of the past, and afraid to live today. He remembered himself as a young boy who was still capable of dreaming those glorious dreams of being someone important, a pilot, doctor or even a policeman.

Today he was afraid to dream. He did not realize they had already taken his dreams. In fact, they'd beat his dreams right out of him.

All people need to feel there is some purpose, some meaning in their life. We would drift endlessly through life without attachment, without trying to build something better for our families or community. I remember as a young boy watching my mother and father drinking. I swore I would never become a drunk like my parents. I thought that by sheer determination I could somehow change the course of my destiny, simply through knowledge. Yet before I realized, I had grown up and in my early teens had become just as substance-addicted as my parents.

How could I explain to myself that I lived when my friends had died such a tragic death? I had already felt terrible guilt over that. How could I live when I could serve no useful purpose?

It wasn't until I found sobriety that I learned that my experience could benefit others. It was then I began to feel my life could have purpose. That purpose was to help others find healing through my personal experience. This sense of purpose became the central aspect of my life. It became the replacement for the sense of isolation and shame that had plagued me all through life. In homes organized around a dysfunction, survival is paramount, and defining a purpose is something that is not a priority on the survival list.

It is the responsibility of the community to ensure that its members have the opportunity to come to know their purpose. By having elders and ceremonies available to our young, we can help them understand instead of feeling confused about their future.

Although the role in life they will play is important, defining how they will relate to others is more significant. By ensuring there is stability and consistency in families, our young people can explore their talents and find their place in society.

By not supporting the efforts of our young, whether it be at school, work, or home, we can help them feel apart of a great circle known as Anishinabe. By believing in them and giving them a say in their future, we can forgo shame and create pride. By recognizing we are good enough without having to prove it, we will heal and use our experiences to help others.

While I was using alcohol and drugs, I never bothered thinking about my purpose or my future. I drifted from place to place, person to person, situation to situation, crisis to crisis. I never thought of my future because my future seemed too bleak and terrifying. I thought alcohol and drugs would eventually kill me so I shied away from thinking about my future. I feared it and continued to drink in order to avoid dealing with its reality.

It wasn't until I received treatment in 1977 for alcohol and drug abuse that I developed the courage to look at my future. During my entire time of substance abuse, I always wondered why I had survived the gas-sniffing experience I discussed in the first chapter of this book. Once I began to deal with the effects of that night, I began to think there had to be some reason for my surviving it. I thought maybe I could reach out to others who experience similar traumas.

The self-help group I was attending helped me to figure out this purpose. It encouraged us to share our stories with those who were still using alcohol. I started to help other people. I told my story in front of other alcoholics. I saw that people could relate to what I was saying, and I felt good about it. I began to feel good about me. I believe it was because I started to help other people that began to change from a self-centred person to one who had genuine concern for others. The process of getting out of myself and reaching out to others presented a different life goal. Instead of worrying so much about my own sobriety, I helped others come to understand the impact of alcohol on their lives and the lives of those they love.

As I journeyed down this path towards discovery of an identity and purposefulness in life, I realized that my vision gave me an important responsibility. One of the important tasks of Sturgeon people is teaching, and I am a member of the Sturgeon Clan. By getting to know my clan and the history of my community, I have developed a sense of continuity. In other words, the history of my family, community, and nation has given me a sense of security.

When I started to do this healing work, I had no idea to which clan I belonged, nor did I know the important role my clan played. It came as a surprise that I had been doing the teaching required of my clan before I knew of my clan role. For some reason, I *was* fulfilling my purpose. All I needed to do was to stay quiet, listen, and ask for guidance from the elders and the Creator.

Values: A Community Responsibility

Bill's Story

I grew up on a reserve in northwestern Ontario in the 1970s. All around me, I saw people drinking and all kinds of violence. I thought this was normal. When I entered into my teen years, the way I solved my problems or dealt with my feelings was to drink or fight. I never knew it was wrong to do those things. No matter where I turned, I saw drunks all around me. I later thought I was nothing but a no good, drunken Indian. I valued little, and I never allowed myself to care about anything or anyone. When I saw how others lived, I began to hate my own people because I thought we were weak. In that process, I began to hate myself. I valued only those things which I thought would help me forget who I was or would numb the shame and hurt I felt deep inside.

I learned to value money, drugs, and sex. I thought these were the things that made one successful, what made me a man. All my self-worth was built on external things that brought gratification. No gratification came from within. Inside I began to believe

*myself to be worthless, someone who would never amount to any-
thing.*

*I believed in all those voices still echoing through my mind. The
things I valued were a reflection of what I saw while growing up. I
valued Jack Daniel more than my own father: Jack Daniel made
me feel strong, confident, and special. All my father ever made me
feel was useless and angry. All my community made me feel was
ashamed. Our community had so much poverty – and so many
intractable problems.*

After working in many First Nations communities, I have come
to believe that Anishinabe people, similar to other tribal societies, have a strong sense of community. When that community is
going through difficult and often traumatic times, the effect on
its members is devastating.

In the above story, Bill talks about the shame he feels being
associated not only with his family but also with his community
and his nation. His sense of hopelessness seems to be enmeshed
with the hopelessness of his community. From the story, we can
see that among Anishinabe people self-worth and values are
often reflected in the physical appearance and priorities of the
community.

I have conducted workshops on community healing in many
different First Nations. One of the concerns often expressed is
why native people do not take better care of their children and
their property. The answer to this question can be best answered
from a historical and cultural perspective.

First of all, natives do not own their own homes. It has only
been recently that the Canada Mortgage and Housing Corporation has given loans to First Nations to secure property. These
loans have to be guaranteed by the band and the band has an
interest on the houses. But in actuality, the band member can
never truly own the house or the land on which it is situated.
Although it has not in the past been in us to value things that
were material, this is now rapidly changing. Many of our people
are beginning to value material things, creating class distinctions
within our First Nations. Instead of equality and homogeneity,

we see poor and well-to-do people within our communities. As a result, many of our people feel isolated and alienated.

It wasn't until much later in life that I began to appreciate what my community meant to me, for a community is more than a place. It is part of my history. It is part of me, a part I could not deny or run away from. It was my connection to Mother Earth and the Creator.

In the world of the Anishinabe, an identity is formed through communion with the community: historically the survival of the community was as important as the survival of the individual.

Wahsheen was an Ojibway man from a fairly isolated northern community. All his life, he lived and worked in his community. At a conference, Wahsheen met a beautiful girl named Beth, who was from a community six hours from his own. As the relationship grew, they decided to get married. Both Wahsheen and Beth loved each other very much. Wahsheen finally decided to leave his job and his community to be with his love. He moved to Beth's community, where he felt uncomfortable because no one really knew him.

After the marriage and his move, Wahsheen began to feel very lonely for his family and his community. Problems in the relationship began to arise, and everyone assumed the problems were associated with the recent death of his brother. Although this tragic grief issue was still pending, what kept Wahsheen from exploring and processing the grief was Wahsheen's feelings of isolation and loneliness in an environment where he felt no comfort or acceptance. Being Anishinabe, losing his community meant losing a great part of himself. The pain of losing his family and community was so great that Wahsheen became very angry with Beth. Although Wahsheen did not get physical with Beth, he began to manipulate and hurt her with his words and attitude.

No matter how Beth begged and stated her love for Wahsheen, and no matter how much Wahsheen loved Beth, they could not stop their relationship from deteriorating. Eventually Wahsheen and Beth's marriage ended, with both suffering deep wounds. Beth blamed Wahsheen's inability to deal with the loss of his

*brother. Wahsheen believed his pain was due to Beth's not under-
standing him.*

Many of the teachings I have received from elders about values
have been along the lines of family interdependence and family
unification. It is not surprising to hear of native people choosing
to stay at home on the reserve when they could have better
opportunities elsewhere. When someone clearly loves and feels
connected to their family, it is easy to abide by these values
without much internal conflict. But what of those from broken,
blended, or families organized around alcohol or other addictions, families in which members are unable to feel that
connection to family and community?

What we value is reflected to us by the values of the community. In the early days, our communities valued sharing and
cooperation. Many of the decisions we made were by consensus. I argue that we moved away from a community system that
valued the relationships we had with one another to a society
based on what an elder has called a wage-slave economy. As we
began to develop individual ownership, we began to misplace
some of the values that traditionally kept our society interdependent. For those of us who came from homes and communities that could not support our individual growth, we drifted into
dependency and codependency.

What we found lacking in ourselves we tried to find in others.
Our relationships became superficial, with no one allowing anyone to really get to know us. We valued this secrecy as though it
were our protection from forces that could ultimately destroy us,
yet it was that very secrecy which would, in fact, be our destruction. And so we continued to deceive ourselves into believing
the pursuit of material wealth was the answer to the emptiness
within our souls. We developed and nurtured our greed, making
sure no one was more important or had more valuable possessions. Instead of seeing what was good in our own life, we con-
centrated on what others had and hated them for it.

Those values began to transcend our relationships. We
became envious of our siblings and in the process began to

believe everyone was against us, or better than us. Instead of valuing cooperation among our families and communities, we valued competition. And if we failed to live up to our standards, we came down hard on ourselves and on those around us.

But I remember a different time. I remember as a child we had adopted a system of borrowing – one of sharing for the common good. This system ensured everyone had the means to survive from one welfare day to the next. 'Today I may borrow a loaf of bread and tomorrow I may lend you some sugar.' It was a system of borrowing that was an expression of generosity and cooperation.

4
The Healing Journey

My Personal Journey

The healing that took place in my family reminds me of a Hopi
prophecy of 1830 which read:

OUR PEOPLE ARE IN THEIR MIDNIGHT
WE WILL COME INTO THE DAYLIGHT AND BECOME LEADERS
WHEN THE EAGLE LANDS ON THE MOON.

Many of us believe the process of healing for aboriginal people
also began in 1969, when Neil Armstrong's lunar vehicle
touched down on the moon for the first time and sent the message that the *Eagle*, had landed.

In our family, this process started with my mother over
twenty years ago. For us, my parents' entry 'into daylight' was as
important as Neil Armstrong's historic landing on the moon. It
did not receive any press coverage, but for us it symbolized a
new life destined to improve the lives of many people, including
those yet unborn. From one seed sprang new generations of
siblings who spoke of healing and growth instead of denial and
shame.

As I mentioned earlier, both my parents were alcoholics. I
believe strongly if it had not been for the alcoholism both would
have been excellent role models. In the same manner, I believe

there are many other parents who could be great parents if they, too, did not become consumed with the substance abuse and addictions associated with growing up in a family organized around pain.

To deal with the pain of rejection and feelings of inadequacy, by the time I was twelve I was abusing the chemicals which eventually led to my alcoholism. At age twelve, my choice of chemical was gasoline because it was easily accessible, and the 'high' I experienced allowed me to forget who I was and where I lived.

I can remember seeing my father working at the sawmill. All ten of us children were very proud of the fact that he worked every day. In those days, I spent a great deal of time with my friends. In many ways, they were also my family. I relied on them for the caring I did not receive when my mom and dad were drinking. Like many other kids, we spent every summer swimming, playing ball, and just goofing off. Unlike many other kids, we also spent a lot of time throwing rocks at cars, drinking, and sniffing gasoline.

Most weekends were spent wondering what kind of weekend it would be. Would it be one of those sober weekends where we would be like a normal family, or would it be a drunken weekend where everything and everyone seemed crazy. I remember the inconsistency being the worst feeling in the world. It felt like we were either going to be in hell or in heaven.

It was those sober weekends that meant the most to me. Those were the times when my father would take the family to our little shack on Haymarsh Bay. As a family, we usually spent those weekends swimming and fishing. More important, it meant my parents would be spending the weekend with us. I loved it when my parents were home. I guess that is why it hurt so much when they were away drinking. When they drank, it meant that we had to deal with the fighting, crying, screaming, and terrifying sounds of drunken partying. It also meant I would spend a better part of the evening worrying. I worried because my parents were not home, and then worried because when they did come home other drunks usually came with them. I was never really sure what was worse, waiting and worrying or listening to the sounds of the drinking.

During the times my father was sober, he was very quiet. When he drank, he became the opposite. At night, when I would be trying to sleep, he would come and talk to me. It was a type of father that I could not truly appreciate.

Yet despite his drunkenness, it was at those times I learned about women, the world, sports, and the way he really felt inside. He talked about his fears, dreams, failures, and frustrations, and tried during these talks to give me some direction for my own life. It was the only time when my father could actually say he loved me. As I look back today, I can see how it was the only way my father could express his true inner feeling. But a child doesn't really understand those things; instead of trying to accept my father's need for intimacy, I learned to resent his midnight intrusions.

My mother was a product of the Catholic school and my father the product of the residential school system. Instead of learning appropriate discipline, my parents were taught to use corporal punishment as a means of control and discipline. At that time, spankings were not considered inappropriate discipline. In fact, the religious community considered you a bad parent if you did not discipline your children by 'spanking.' The not too silent code of spare the rod and spoil the child was very much a society value.

In my earlier years, I didn't see anyone trying to teach my parents new parental skills. What I did see was the confirmation that hitting was allowable as an appropriate means of discipline. But regardless of society values or the intentions, the feeling associated with the spankings remained the same. It always made one feel humiliation and indignity.

This was reinforced at school, where corporal punishment as a means of control and discipline was also the choice. For the slightest infraction of the rules, you would be disciplined with a wide range of tactics, ranging from shaming rituals, in which children were forced to stand in the corner of the room for long periods of time, to being ridiculed in front of the class by having to sit on a stool, or being sent directly to the principal's office. Being sent to the principal's office usually meant getting strapped with a leather strap with a texture similar to a beaver's tail.

I could never decipher if the violation was consistent with the punishment. It was more likely the degree of punishment coincided with the mood of the principal. I did know that I was always deeply afraid of being punished. Yet I always did my best to put on the a brave front. I did not want anyone to think I was a cry baby.

You might feel a hatred for the teacher; however, being brought up Catholic meant you were the one who was bad. No matter what people did to me, I was apparently the one who was in the wrong. I was taught to believe I was born defective, with original sin on my soul. Of course, that meant all I had to do to be bad was to be born. It was not very helpful in trying to develop some kind of sense of self-worth. My self-worth had to come from outside myself.

School was supposed to be a place of learning, growth, and development, but for me it only presented a different set of problems. The only similarity between home and school was the feeling of anger it generated because I was not as good as the other kids. My clothes usually had patches, my lunch consisted of mustard sandwiches, and my body usually was dirty. Being called a 'dirty Indian' brought forth anger and hatred for the system that was supposed to teach me. Because of this, I never really developed a commitment to education. My education came from home, and I was a prize pupil.

It was not surprising to have all kinds of drunks come to my house after the bars closed. From my bed at the back of the house, I could tell by the voices whether violence was going to break out. I still feel sadness when I think of my mother, who was too drunk to protect her children from those who came there, yet I know this was all part and parcel of the drinking. It was her alcoholism that dictated whether she could or would do anything about the drunks who came into the room.

Most people I knew never drank for just a single night. Instead everyone I knew drank for the entire weekend. Those weekends I usually ate raw porridge mixed with water while stepping over and watching the drunks who were passed out half-clothed. By Saturday the house was a mess, with beer and wine spilled all over the floor. Mixed with the dirt from people's shoes, it made the floor sticky, so sticky that my socks would stick to the floor.

I remember a great deal of violence. I remember drunks fighting drunks, brothers fighting brothers, women fighting other women, men beating their wives, and wives beating their husbands. I watched the fights. I saw the blood spilling from the faces of drunks. I watched until all the action was over, and then I would go back to bed as if nothing happened. I prayed no one would hurt my dad and was at the same time afraid he would hurt someone. I was always afraid something bad would happen and I would end up being alone. It was a feeling that never left me.

I hated my parents' drinking. I became confused and thought that meant I hated. *them*. I couldn't imagine what kind of child would have the boldness to hate his parents. I thought there must be something wrong with me. Maybe if I could be a better son, a better brother, or a better student, things would change.

In my confusion, I trusted a boy who was six years older than the eight I had already lived. His name was Marcel, and he was also the only older person who paid genuine attention to me. Marcel often gave me snuff, making me feel grown up and special. Snuff was a tobacco product you placed between your gum and lower lip. Instead of smoking cigarettes, snuff gave you the effect of smoking without actually smoking. I hated the taste of snuff, but I loved the acceptance it gave me. The bad taste was a small price to pay for the attention of someone I admired. I pretended to enjoy it.

Marcel was a sexual perpetrator, but at that time I did not think of him as an abuser. I cared deeply for Marcel. I guess that is why it hurt so much when later in life I realized what he had done had left me damaged. The abuse happened on a Friday evening when my parents were out drinking. I remember feeling sad because I knew my father would be drinking for the weekend, which meant our fishing trip would be cancelled. I went over to see Marcel, who always seemed happy to see me. The one thing I knew about Marcel was that whenever he said he would do something I knew he would do it. We sat around and talked for about an hour. He asked me if he could rub my back because my muscles were tense.

As he was massaging my back, he reached around and touched my penis. I jumped up from the floor and started to pull my T-shirt back on. He reached over and grabbed me, kissing me on the lips. I wanted to run away, but he placed his hand on the back of my head and held it to his chest. I started to cry, and as he tenderly stroked my head, the tears came from my eyes. I thought I would never be able to stop crying. After I cried, I also felt a great comfort. For the first time in my life, I felt someone other than my brothers and sisters, someone older, cared about me. It was at that time that I decided that I would do almost anything to feel the way he made me feel.

I never felt shame or remorse, but I knew that if anyone found out I would be ridiculed. Almost daily through out that summer, I was a willing participant with Marcel. No matter how painful the sexual abuse was, it could not be as painful as believing my friends would think me defective, different, or damaged. So the abuse continued until Marcel and his family moved away. It was a dichotomy: in some ways, I was sad to see him go, but I was also happy to see the end. I wanted Marcel to love and care for me, and I did anything to make sure he did. I found it difficult to face my friends, and I prayed that no one would ever find out about what had happened, that this secret would go to the grave with me.

I loved to swim and run logs down by the sawmill with my friends. There was a group of us who my sister would fondly refer to as the Four Musketeers. So it was, the four of us standing in our little world, constantly dreaming of leaving and finding a better life. There were many times when we would lie on the dock at the sawmill dreaming those visions of fame and fortune. Individually we dared not, but as a group we dared to dream about being something other than held to the reserve.

I was sexually abused for the second time when I was ten years

old. One of my cousins and I were collecting pop bottles to sell at
the air base located near the residential school. At that time, the
residential school was being torn down to make room for a new
one. The school was abandoned. The workers who were to tear it
down had yet to arrive. As we were walking by, a man I knew
offered to buy the pop bottles off of us for more money than
what we would have gotten at the air base. He told us to put the
bottles inside one of the abandoned classrooms, which we
quickly did. Just as we were about to leave, the man grabbed me
and told me to stay. All of a sudden, more people entered into
the room and formed a circle around us. What happened next
was almost beyond belief.

They told us to take off our clothes. We did so, and suddenly
one of the men grabbed me and forced me face down onto one
of the old tables placed against the wall. He then undid his pants
and began his sexual assault. I remember feeling powerless. I
also remember a fear so terrifying it felt like I was about to die.
When he was finished, another man grabbed my hair and pulled
me towards him. He whispered to me that he would kill me if I
didn't do exactly what he said.

He undid his pants and told me to put his penis in my mouth.
I almost vomited because I was so disgusted by what was happening. Yet fear caused me to do exactly what he asked. I must
have blacked out – because the next thing I remember was my
cousin and me walking away from the building. Neither of us
mentioned this incident to anyone. The experience left a lasting
impression on me, an impression that would last a lifetime. I
walked away disgusted with myself.

By the time I turned twelve years old, I was still emotionally
numb. Everything that happened in my life served only to validate my mistrust. I lived in fear that someone would find out
about me. I felt that somehow I was touched by the hand of the
devil himself. It was becoming more difficult to live with what
happened.

I found my escape in solvent. I discovered the fantasy and dis-
association sniffing gas can bring. I relished this escape. I sought
it as often and as much as I could. For me, sniffing gas repre-

sented freedom from my pain. I did not care about anything but getting caught. Gasoline became my greatest friend, one that brought me gifts, the gifts of fantasy and escape. It was my first love, and I loved it with all my heart. I sought its relief and planned my life around it.

I remember the day that would shape my life forever. It was 1 July 1967, Canada's one hundredth birthday, and some friends and I were looking forward to ending the celebrations by sniffing gas in an old abandoned car. Our parents were also out celebrating, and we knew their drinking would last a couple of days. After spending the day in Fort Frances, we returned to the reserve. We stole five gallons of gas from the tractor at the lumber mill on the reserve, hiding the gasoline in the car. We then went for a swim and agreed to meet after dark.

Around 9:00 that evening, I left for the old car. As darkness approached, my friends and I found some old cans which we used to hold the gas. All we had to do then was sniff the gas and enjoy the hallucinations. I am not sure how a candle got into the car, but in my stupor I remember looking up and thinking how pretty it looked with its light dancing on the dashboard. Around 11:00 that night, I went home, leaving two of my friends still sniffing gasoline. As I came around the front of the car, I saw the two faces looking out at me. I waved goodbye to them.

Around midnight the car exploded from the buildup of gasoline fumes and the candle. My two best friends died, killed as a direct result of sniffing gasoline. It left the families and community trying to determine what went wrong. It was an experience that would shape the rest of my life.

The following days were like a fog. I fought to hold back my tears. As the days passed, I remember the funeral. The coffins were closed, and in my childlike mind I believed my friends were not in them. For days after the funeral, I would go search for them. I went to all the places where we used to play, down to the old sawmill where we spent hours and hours playing cowboys and Indians, then up to the sawdust pile, the old swimming hole, and finally to their homes.

No matter where I looked, the day always ended in the same

way. I walked silently home. On my birthday, only eleven days after my friends had died in the car, my sisters, out of their love and concern for me, held a birthday party. This was the first real birthday party I remember having – and the only guests who came were my brothers and sisters.

Right after my thirteenth birthday, I was subpoenaed to the courthouse to testify at the inquest into their deaths. Nothing I could possibly think of could have prepared me for what was about to happen. As I entered the courthouse, I found a large, cold place. I began to feel afraid, wondering if they thought I had killed my friends. As the proceedings went on, I was finally called to the witness box.

Although the inquest laid no guilt, I walked out of that building condemning myself. In my thirteen-year-old mind, I believed I had killed both my friends. I walked away wishing it was I who had died in the car.

I never really recovered from their deaths, and carried the burden of guilt far into adulthood. For the following four years, my life remained the same, with the exception that I was beginning to grow up. By the time I had reached seventeen, the effects of that experience were buried deep inside me. I don't recall much about those years other than a great deal of sadness and aloneness. I later remember coming out of my gigantic fog. It was as though someone had erased most of my life.

I also remember my fear. It is the one feeling I can describe easily. But that fear changed the day I had my first drink of alcohol. I'll never forget how I got started. I was seventeen, in high school, and heading into the washroom when another student, a friend of mine from Manitou Rapids reserve, asked me if I wanted a drink of lemon gin. I first didn't think it a good idea. I had seen what alcohol had done to my parents. In spite of my apprehension, I'll never forget the feeling I had when the gin took effect. Although I disliked the taste, the feeling spreading through my body was unmistakably pleasant. From the first time I took a drink, it seemed as though my whole world had suddenly changed. At last, I had found a friend and did not feel as though I was alone any more.

My fear subsided, and I felt I had a kind of control over my life. For the first time, I did not feel apprehensive. I was able to talk to people. I went up to a girl and initiated a conversation. I was amazed at the ease with which I spoke. Increasingly, I found my conversation flowed quite easily – I was even witty, charming, charismatic. I am not sure if others noticed my change in personality, but I sure felt it. I was confident and thought I could take on the whole world. My new-found confidence was only because the alcohol had made me feel brave, yet I did not care what caused it. I only wanted to continue feeling that way.

At first I thought drinking a lot of fun. I found companionship with the other teens who drank, and they seemed to understand me. I was finally part of a group, a feeling I had not experienced since I was thirteen. Alcohol helped me forget about all the things that had happened to me.

But by the time I was twenty, I had attempted suicide a number of times. Somewhere along the line, alcohol had stopped making me feel good. I would wake up in the morning not knowing what I had done the night before. I hated not knowing what I was doing, but the numbness alcohol provided outweighed the consequences. Somehow I just rationalized that things would improve – all I had to do was find the right combination of drinks.

In my attempts to normalize my drinking, I tried many forms of geographical cures. I moved to the city of Thunder Bay, Ontario, and back to Fort Frances when it didn't work out there. The problem was that no matter where I went, I always took myself with me. Slowly it was beginning to dawn on me that perhaps I was the problem. As my drinking progressed, I became increasingly demoralized. I felt like there was no way out. Even my best friend, King Alcohol, no longer provided relief. With the added burden caused by the shame over the things I did and the people I hurt while I was drinking, I felt no reason to continue living. Whenever I looked into the mirror, I knew I had become what I had never wanted to be – one of the drunks who use to frequent my home.

I knew I was in deep trouble when I woke up one morning

with a loaded rifle in the bed with me. As I thought back to the night before, I vaguely remembered putting the gun to my head, pulling the hammer back, releasing it, and starting the process all over again. Sometime during the night, I finally fell asleep with the gun still in a firing position. I knew if I didn't do something about my drinking, I would die.

While I was going through this, my mother found sobriety through a twelve-step, self-help program. As she learned to appreciate sobriety, she began to practise tough love on my father. After her return from treatment, she had left my father, who was still drinking. It worked. Once my father realized my mother was serious about her sobriety and that he might lose her, he agreed to pursue treatment.

The dream of every child of an alcoholic is to have his parents sober, but I was still very sick and could not appreciate what they had done. Having acquired two sober parents, all of my visits back home consisted of them warning me about the 'disease' called alcoholism and encouraging me to get treatment. They believed that I, too, was an alcoholic.

I disliked what they were telling me and interpreted what they were saying as evangelism. But despite my resistance, it wasn't long before I began to see how most of my present problems had come from my drinking. Each time I saw my parents, they seemed happier than I ever remember. It was through their example that this recovery stuff began to interest me.

The Individual's Road to Assuming Responsibility

One night in July of 1977, everything seemed to fall apart. I found myself constantly drinking in spite of my parents' attempts to make me see the light. I was getting so drunk that I would lose my memory after only three beers. This was followed by feelings of depression, hopelessness, and fear of impending doom. I knew that if I continued along that path I would eventually kill myself.

One night I'd had enough and called my father to come pick me up. All I remember was having the last bit of alcohol I had poured down the drain. That night my father didn't preach to me and tell me things that I already knew; instead he told me he understood. A friend of his came and talked to me for most of the night, and for some reason that particular night I believed what this man was telling me. For the first time in my life, I began to trust someone.

The following week, I started attending a few self-help meetings. I unfortunately did not find myself remaining sober for very long. But finally in September 1977, after countless failed attempts to stay clean and sober, I entered a drug and alcohol treatment centre in Thunder Bay. I found my way out of the chaos because someone in my family had found a way to end the cycle of addiction in their own life. In other words, by watching my parents enjoy sobriety, I began to believe there was hope for me. If alcoholism is generational, then it only stands to reason that recovery can also be generational.

I had to begin to accept responsibility for my own alcohol and drug use. No longer could I blame my parents. No one had forced me to drink. It was I who held the bottle to my lips and tilted it back.

The first step in this recovery process was accepting the fact that I had worked very hard to get myself sick enough to not even value my own life. I sought self-esteem by finding acceptance among those whose drinking was also problematic. In the end, the one I hurt the most was myself. Yet I did hurt other people, too and I had to accept responsibility for that by making amends and by becoming a positive role model for others.

To this very day, I haven't taken a drink. I owe a great deal to my parents, whose support and encouragement allowed me a second chance at life. It was a relief to have someone in my life who had already been through the difficult things we have to face when we try and 'get sober' – paying some long-overdue bills, pairing lost or damaged friendships, rebuilding self-respect and broken, tattered lives.

This process of recovery continued within our family. Soon another family member found sobriety, then a sister, followed by four more of my siblings. The recovery process took over ten years, yet it all began with a single family member wanting to change their life.

In spite of virtually nonexistent programs to help people who needed and wanted recovery, a few community members walked toward sobriety and remained clean and sober. From that small number, many of our community people are now in recovery and are receiving ongoing support from the same self-help program that had saved my life. It all started with just *a few people* who shared the same vision of sobriety. I don't believe I would be here today were it not for those few people who had the dedication and commitment to keep those early self-help meetings going.

Anishinabe people need to heal within the structure of the family and community. When we start our healing journey, we need not only to consider the family and community in healing but also to *involve* them in the process. Sometimes our families may still be 'stuck' within their own issues. How, then, can we go to our father and ask for support for our abuse of alcohol when he himself is caught up in the cycle of addiction?

As a young person growing up in a family where some of the members had not yet begun their healing journey, I had to rely solely on my parents as my primary means of support. After treatment I began attending a self-help group that my mother had been going to for years. In time, however, I began to feel there was something missing. I didn't feel as if I truly belonged to the group. Despite everyone's attempt to make me feel welcome, I still felt at a distance to people. I had a difficult time letting my down my defences enough for people to get to know me.

I realized that I could not complete the circle without going back and discovering my own identity – discovering who I was as a complete person. This search for my identity meant I had to stop denying my Anishinabe ancestry and believing that the mainstream ways of healing had all the answers. Although I am grateful to my many teachers and counsellors who have helped me along the way, I ultimately had to take responsibility and complete the final journey myself.

I began to attend ceremonies and pow wows. I spoke to and

learned from our elders about our Anishinabe ways. When comfortable enough, I brought tobacco to an elder and asked to receive my spirit name. Eventually, I began to feel comfortable with my own identity. As I listened at healing and talking circles, my fear of being Anishinabe began to evaporate. In the end, I was no longer ashamed of my past. I was *proud* of my Anishinabe ancestry.

I have always heard people talking about wholistic healing but have come to realize that until we make healing *all-inclusive* by including men, families, and communities, our attempts at healing will always fall short of their mark. To feel complete as a person, I also had to begin dealing with my sexual abuse as a child. One of the problems I had encountered was that there were no support groups for men who were victims of child sexual abuse. I realized that the system was designed to see men as offenders, with very little programming directed to the victimization of men. And for that reason, I had to go through that healing process by myself. For wholistic healing to be a reality, healing must be *all-inclusive*; everyone, including men, need to be part of the healing process. As Anishinabe people, we can all relate on some level to the victimization of those who have been oppressed. We still are, to some degree, victims of the dominant culture.

This concept of *all-inclusiveness* goes beyond the present definition of mind, body, and spirit as it takes into account everyone within the family, community, and society. The Besante model of family healing that has been described in the previous chapters of this book looks at family as an important element in healing and moves beyond to include the community in the healing process. Without community responsibility, we will continue to fall short in our efforts to reach out to our neighbours still suffering from the effects of alcohol and other traumas. If we are to speak about wholism, we must move beyond talk and incorporate accountability and community into our programs and services.

Using this simple definition, we are now able to view the entire picture. A wholistic family healing model based on responsibility would, then, look like Figure 6.

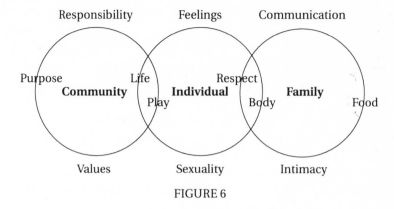

FIGURE 6

Notice from this model that the circles are interconnected, indicating the importance of maintaining the connection between the individual, family, and community. In the middle circle, we see the areas of responsibility for the individual in relation to the family and the community. The individual is responsible for his/her feelings, body, sexuality, and breath, as discussed in Chapter 1. When we fail to assume responsibility for ourselves, we drift into indifference by blaming everyone else for the way we feel. We transfer those same messages to our children, and the cycle of blame continues from one generation to the next.

Denial becomes a way of life for children of alcoholic parents. I hadn't realized just how often I unconsciously distorted the truth. I grew up believing that drinking parties lasting from Friday night to Sunday afternoon were normal. I believed this because everyone I knew and was friends with in my community did the same thing. Growing up in a community where everyone I knew drank led me to believe that all people drank, and drank to excess. I thought it was *normal* to have parties start out with lots of laughter and later turn into bloody fights, desperate cries, and sounds of breaking glass. Never did I suspect that anyone grew up without such sights.

Not until later in adolescence did I realize there were some families who played, listened, and spoke kindly to each other. I was astonished to find families whose time spent together was filled with joy and laughter.

The Family's Road to Assuming Responsibility for Its Members

As I was going through the final stages of alcoholism, my family had also entered into a new era of healing. It began with my mother, who had always been the true leader in our family.

When she first sobered up in 1975, my mother's wish was to die sober. On 22 October 1995, my mother passed away, having achieved sobriety for over twenty years. The greatest gift she gave me was life, and she did so twice, the day of my birth, and the day in 1977 when she drove me to a treatment centre in Thunder Bay.

It is not surprising that within the aboriginal community women play such an important role in the healing of the family. When our women are still stuck in their own pain, the effects can be felt by individual members of the family and community. Women need to recognize the importance of their role and the importance they play in the lives of the community. As well, men need to recognize the importance of our women. No longer can we teach our young men to disrespect our women. From a very early age, we must teach our men that our culture will only be as strong as our women.

I was travelling back from a northern First Nation with a prominent elder one day in 1993. It was my pleasure to ride with him for over six hours. As we travelled, we spoke of many things, including the role of women and medicine. As he spoke of the strength of our women and how the role of women was changing within the culture, I asked him what kind of medicine (sacred herbs used for healing and purifying) were for women. In his kindest and gentlest voice, he leaned over to me, and touching my shoulder said, 'young man, women are the medicine.'

As I thought about his words, I couldn't help but think of the importance of the women in my life. For the first time, I saw the role of our women through different eyes. No longer would I view women as second-class citizens. I was able to see that whenever I put a woman down I was putting myself down, for I am a product of my mother, and for me to be a healthy human being I must respect that part of myself which is my mother. I endeavour to be more sensitive to the inequality that prevails in our society. My healing encourages me to speak out against wife assault and other forms of violence against woman.

In aboriginal society, men and women are healing in the same circle. Although it is the aboriginal way, men and women should not be in the same circle until each has worked through their own sexuality issues. Both must feel comfortable with each other in order to heal together. When a man is hurt by a woman, sometimes only a woman can help the man complete the cycle of healing; however, it is the helper's responsibility to ensure the healing takes place on a spiritual as opposed to a physical level.

Unfortunately, we have listened to the mainstream view of male and female roles. We believe them when they tell us that women are subservient to men. All too often, we see women as our possessions, when in reality women are the real leaders. Without their ability to bring forth life, our whole society would cease to exist. I have witnessed over the past twenty years women leading their husbands and their children into healing. This was definitely the case in my family.

After entering treatment, when I looked at my family I began to see my parents in a different light. I began to see what they were doing with their recovery. For the first time, I felt a deep sense of admiration and respect for them. Slowly it began to filter into my mind that recovery was possible. Over the course of that summer, I began to think if they could do it then maybe I could. I began to think maybe they were right.

Recovery for my family was a process. By witnessing the recovery of my mother, I was able to demonstrate sobriety to my siblings by being a positive role model. I do not believe our young people will listen to us when we talk about the ravages of alcoholism and other social ills. Instead they will be watching to see how we demonstrate healing in our day to day lives. I demonstrated sobriety by staying sober. It wasn't surprising, then, to see other siblings in my family look towards recovering from family issues and substance abuse. This created a whole new way of looking at things and a whole new way of relating to one another. No longer did we feel the need to pretend that we had the perfect family.

As a family, we were very lucky because our mother chose to show and teach us about sobriety through her actions and not her words. In this way, our mother was the medicine our family so desperately needed. As a result of her courage and determination, her children were able to enjoy what every child of alcoholic parent dream of – sober parents.

She took her role as mother seriously and stood beside her children through their own weaknesses and near-death experiences with alcoholism and codependency. Of course, tempers still flared. But the difference now was that all of my family members knew a great love for each other.

In recovery, we began to respect our parents for the work they did in providing us with two lives, one at birth and the other in sobriety. We began to share a common bond with each other. Those in recovery became the keepers of those painful memories of each family member and the valuable contributions each made during those early days of childhood survival. It felt as if we had lived two lives.

We had lost much in childhood because of alcoholism, yet we had gained far more in recovery. The endless bouts with depression, anger, confusion, rage, shame, self-doubt, and apathy have become our greatest teachers. The greatest gift we can give our families and our children is ourselves. Our greatest challenge will be to continue to be our real selves in the face of uncertainty and discord.

The test of our recovery will be how we feel each morning as we stare at the person reflected back in the mirror. If we can look at ourselves with confidence and love, this will be passed to our children. When we view life in this light, we see the ability to change and end family violence within our power.

The Community's Road to Assuming Responsibility for Its Members

Aboriginal people appreciate that our communities need to be involved in the healing process. Yet there are many who do not understand the traditional ways, nor do they understand what it means to be aboriginal. Much of our self-worth and identity comes to us through our identification with our communities. As our communities heal and change, so will their value systems.

Strong leadership is the key factor in healing our communities. Without strong leadership, those who are willing to face the realities of our situation will continue to be lost. We are in the midst of overcoming six generations of oppression which have left our families in shambles, our young men without vision, our old men without wisdom, our women without power, and our children without a future. Facing this is paramount in bringing those still lost into healing. Our families need to relearn many of the things they have been taught about ourselves and our parenting. We need to recognize that within our communities lie the answers to all of our hardships and that *recognizing* those hardships is the first step towards community healing.

When a hurricane comes and tears down our buildings, uproots our trees, destroys our water supply, and cripples our children, it is not enough to say 'Finally the sun is out. I can't see anything wrong now.' Instead of taking a short-sighted view of the damage, we must survey it, acknowledge what the hurricane has done, empathize with and help those who are crippled, bury our dead, ensure the safety of the survivors, and begin to repair the harm caused by the hurricane. Our leadership must begin to address issues through an honest sharing of concern. Community members must begin to take part in that process, and our leaders need to hear what the members of their communities are saying.

Within First Nations communities, there is a tremendous expectation for our leadership to be able to deal with many different types of situations. We expect our caregivers to be advanced crisis interventionists who can deal with a wide variety of crises.

Recently one of our chiefs was quoted as saying that his community did not have a suicide problem because his people had taken a suicide training course. This alone is not the answer. The answer lies within the community's ability to provide each member with a sense of purpose and a reason for living. As leaders, it is our responsibility to ensure that each of our community members has the opportunity to acquire the skills necessary for long-term employment. By providing long-term solutions for employment opportunities, our community members can reach towards self-sufficiency.

I began work with a native organization given a mandate to provide information on health and family violence to twenty-four First Nations within the Province of Ontario. We started our work as a project conducting community development workshops in those twenty-four communities. As we progressed, we were able to form a corporation and apply for funding to provide more services to First Nations. The project flourished.

In 1995 the residents of Ontario elected a government whose sole intent was to reduce and/or eliminate the provincial budget deficit. In order to fulfil this mandate, social programs were cut across the province. The organization I worked for had one of those programs. We lost employees who provided community development and training in family violence.

We have gone on, however. As I continued to plan a strategy towards self-sufficiency, noted that many of the First Nations were not equipped to access our service through the World Wide Web or Internet. I proposed to the board of directors that we offer that service to people at cost. The service would provide and maintain home pages on the Internet, software development, computer installation, and provide any training people needed on computer programs.

The second part of the strategy was to develop curriculum on healing principles which could be used towards credit for university and colleges courses. The curriculum would also be used for hands-on training of caregivers in the communities.

The third component of the self-sufficiency plan was to create a newspaper promoting articles, people, agencies, and programs, which would shed positive light on native people. Many aboriginal people are concerned that the only news written about them is negative. This paper would do two things: generate income for programs and create a positive atmosphere for aboriginal people. Further, by contracting research projects through this newspaper, we would produce more accurate information about our people. The money raised through these initiatives has the potential to make the organization self-sufficient if it is supported by the communities.

What started as a project in the basement of a band hall has been developed into a corporation that will see some degree of self-sufficiency within four years. This is a great example of economic and social development working cooperatively within the same framework and a kind of community initiative that needs to be created and supported by our people.

Combating Community Denial

Historically community denial has served its purpose. In the 1970s, if we told anyone that sexual or physical abuse was taking place within our communities, the Children's Aid Society would come in and take our children away. Community denial was clearly a survival tactic.

We have only begun to demonstrate our courage by rejecting disavowal and facing the truth. When we create programs and services helping our families, we are creating an atmosphere in which our community members can feel safe and good about themselves. Instead of looking at our social safety network as a symbol of our need to heal, we must look at it as *our healing*. The creation of a social network helps us to view our communities in a more positive light. It lets members who are still suffering from the effects of oppression and assimilation know there is a way out whenever it is wanted. Social programs create a change in the value system. We begin to tell the world that we as a community value the healing of our members. It does no one any good if we stand up and pretend nothing is wrong. The only ones we hurt are those who really need the services.

While working on a project, I came across an article about a community that had constructed a sign placed at a road entering into the community. That sign clearly stated the community's policy on family violence, that this community would not tolerate family violence of any form. It told community members that the community valued healing and created a need to address outstanding needs of support victims and offenders of family violence.

For the formation of community policy to be effective, the community had to look at a way to address violators and victims. To do this, they addressed five key areas.

1. Finding ways to reach out to those still suffering from violence, addictions, eating disorders, loss of identity, purposelessness, hopelessness, anger, disdain, and suicide.
2. Developing plans to ensure people are able to feel safe in discussing issues of family violence and healing – such things as safe homes, removing offenders from the community for the safety of the victims, and legal issues concerning the police.
3. Looking at ways to help individuals heal from trauma and abuse.
4. Looking at ways families can heal from abusive situations and relationships which were/are abusive.
5. Ending the cycle of violence and abuse in our families and communities by looking at ways to *prevent* family violence and other issues.

By addressing all five areas of concern, this community can develop individual and community plans to address those issues and in turn help enhance the quality of life for its members.

Moving beyond Grief

To move beyond grief, we must begin to deal with the losses that have happened in our communities. Beginning in 1830 and finally ending in the 1960s, many of our children were taken away and placed in residential schools. Others were fostered out to non-native homes, and lost touch with their families. My father was sent to a residential school in Fort Frances. He was taken away from his family for ten months of the year. At residential schools, our parents and grandparents learned to either obey the rules while under the strict care of the church – defy them.

I am a second-generation survivor of the residential school. I have felt the effects of the residential school in the losses we experienced from alcoholism and family violence. I have felt it in the loss of my parents' ability to connect with my brothers and sisters on a deep emotional level. My father and mother found it difficult to say those three magic words 'I love you.'

Through the acceptance of our responsibility as individuals, families, and communities, we will come to realize the real meaning of wholism. It will become for us the only way we can heal. This message will be accepted by others who like ourselves could not complete the circle of healing without walking a natural road leading to a deeper self-understanding. Instead of seeing ourselves as people who needed to be *saved* and *rescued,* we need to recognize the importance of the role we will play in the Hopi prophecy mentioned earlier in this chapter.

This new way of viewing ourselves and our willingness to share our wisdom, strength, and faith will be the ground on which new foundations for living will be built – foundations created out of a free gift given to us by the Creator. Those gifts are our ability to love and care for each other. The *interdependency* created through the acceptance of our individual responsibility will enable us to eradicate the ravages created by dependencies and codependencies; both of which have for too long paralysed our families and communities.

How do we make the transformations required to bring about this shift in the way we view healing and life? There is no easy way to bring ourselves to the forefront of healing, but through dedication and commitment, we can build healing for all people. I believe that by relearning some simple concepts and applying them to life, you can accept a resonsibility for yourself that can create a chain reaction of recovery within your family and community. But there is a proviso: don't do it for anyone else but yourself. The only person you can change is *you*.

Recovery is often a slow process to which there are no quick solutions. It took us over six generations to get to the point where we are today – so we need to be patient and settle for small steps on the road to recovery. What is important is the way we measure our progress by our ability to live life to the fullest and our willingness to share our recovery with those who want to hear about it.

We must keep in mind that we have the resource people needed for healing within our individual communities. Our people are survivors, champions, and warriors who have survived an oppression striking at the very core of our spirits. Today our challenge is to accept a new prophecy, one bringing self-fulfilment and self-worth. That prophecy is to accept responsibility for ourselves, and to end the cycle of blame, creating an atmosphere and attitude which promotes and generates healing.

We must look for progress in our recovery and not compare ourselves to others. There are no perfect people so be gentle with your criticism. We will make mistakes, and maybe fall, but we must be willing to get up, shake off the dust, and move on. By expressing our feelings appropriately and not hurting others, we can move on without holding to the past.

5

Into the Daylight: Moving towards Wholism

Frank's Story

I always tried to control everything around me, my wife, my children, my employees, everything. Yet no matter how hard I tried, I always failed in all my attempts to gain control over my life. My whole life has been a vain attempt to have everything my own way. God, half the time I never even realized I did it. All my attempts to keep my wife, the jealousy, the accusations, the pleading meant nothing. She began to despise me because I did not allow her any freedom and trust. I guess it was because I felt so powerless, worthless, and without purpose. I thought anyone could steal her away. Deep inside me, I felt everyone else was better than me and that sooner or later she would figure it out and leave.

You will never understand what it is like to live like that, always afraid, yet trying to prove to myself and everyone else that I was in control of my life, secure and worthy of everything I possessed. I saw everything I had in life as possessions, including my wife and children.

Someone explained to me that spirituality was about letting go of control, and I fought letting go every step of the way. It cost me the love of those I loved most because I built a prison for them and called that love. I tried to build strong walls around those I loved where only I could be in control, and in the process almost destroyed their lives.

My own fear, maybe of being betrayed or abandoned, became their fear vicariously through their love for me. I thought I would die if one more person left me. I guess I did die in some ways when they left. I thank my higher power that I did because when the Creator breathed new life into me that day I surrendered to him.

I knew somehow I was different. I knew my outlook was different. Instead of worrying about me, I began to worry about my children. I wanted to make it up to them. They had it rough growing up with an alcoholic for a father. I pray now. Maybe I don't go to church, but I pray, and I believe God hears me. He must because I'm alive today. I'm alive and I'm grateful for my life.

Maybe I will never completely forgive myself. I guess that is not as important as cleaning up some of the mess I made during those times. I heard an elder say for an Anishinabe to become a healer he must die. I may not have physically died, but I felt like death for years. It was someone's kindness that breathed life into me. I'll never forget it. I'll never forget to be kind.

In most situations, mistrust does not happen overnight. It is usually the result of countless betrayals and inconsistent messages. As a result of those inconsistencies and betrayals, it is very difficult for people to trust in something other than themselves. In my experience, fear is the main block to attaining any degree of spirituality. If we look closely, however, in most cases that fear can turn out to be nothing more than a 'boogyman' with no real power to hurt us. The power that fear has over us lies in the mystical belief that others will think negatively of us or will ultimately let us down. The reality is that people will let us down and disappoint us; however, our reaction to that can be determined by the amount of trust we have in a power inside us. If we are secure in our person, we can overcome all types of obstacles.

The understanding of spirituality and the transformations I made during recovery began with *me*. It all started the day I decided to stop drinking and to enter an alcohol and drug treatment centre. I believe my higher power took care of me when I was using alcohol and drugs because there were many times I should have fared more badly than I did. Yet for some reason, in spite of myself, I had somehow managed to survive grave situations. I have heard this sentiment echoed by many people who travelled the same road of self-destruction.

As I learned more about myself, my life continued to improve. My self-image became more and more positive. As I grew in the twelve-step program, I began to formulate a concept of a power greater than myself. At that time, I chose to call this power God, although I did not really understand the significance of the word. I only knew that something must have cared enough about me to see me through some difficult times. Slowly I began to trust in this power. I also realized I now belonged to a new family or brotherhood that supported and understood me.

It wasn't long before this new brotherhood had allowed me to begin trusting again. Within the confines of this new family, I was able to express ideas, feelings, and experiences that shaped my life without fear of being kicked out or ridiculed. I began to gain respect for myself and for others. I began to see that the world did not revolve around me, but that I was one of many travelling this road called life. Eventually I began to wonder about the beliefs and values of my people. Yet I never really acted on this until I met my wife, Mona-Rose. She challenged me to look at who I was as an Anishinabe. This kind of support was a blessing, because all my life, even in healing and attending self-help meetings, I always thought there was something missing. The reality was that no matter how hard I tried, I could never completely heal using mainstream methods regardless of how similar they were to Anishinabe beliefs and customs .

When I went back and explored my ancestry, I began to feel more connected to my community and my nation. I went into the sweat lodge, and when I announced my name I realized everyone was using their Anishinabe name. I felt hurt and detached because I didn't have a spirit name to announce. This made me feel different from everyone else, but it made me realize I needed to go back to the beginning to find my identity, back to a time before my birth, to a place where the grandfathers knew me as Anishinabe. Although I did not have my spirit name, I was welcomed into the sweat lodge.

Later I brought tobacco to an elder and asked him for my spirit name. He accepted my tobacco and in about six months' time called me and said my name had entered into this world and we should prepare a ceremony and a 'give-away.' The day finally came, and I asked four people to be my sponsors, my aunties and uncles. We prepared a feast and I gladly gave away some of my possessions. It was one of the greatest experiences of my life. For many years, I had always felt I did not belong any-where. Now I felt a part of something, a part of a great family known as Anishinabe.

Before starting on this road, I assumed it would lead to a bet-ter life, or perhaps even to God. What I discovered was that the road really led to me. It led to a greater understanding of all my imperfection, fully equipped with defects and insecurities. It led me to knowing and loving myself despite of those imperfections. On this road, the destination is not what is important. It is the journey itself. When we only focus on reaching our goal, we fail to see the beauty in the journey. Spirituality is the part of you which helps you see the beauty along the way.

My spirituality allows me to see the goodness in you before I see anything else. It is that part of me which asks me to disclose my soul to you and say it's okay when you don't understand. My spirituality is the part leading me to a greater awareness of another manner of living, a world where the ancestors still live, waiting and supporting us on this journey.

Spirituality is not about religion, although in recovery you can choose to follow any sacred belief. Spirituality is concerned with the relationship you have to your greater power regardless of what you call that power. An elder once told me that religion comprised the rules and regulations of how we talked to God, while spirituality was the process and relationship we have with our greater power. This reminded of a story I once heard in my journey to sobriety. It concerned a man who had been drinking for years and had lost his job, his family, and his self-respect.

One day he was trying to stay sober and decided to go to church. On his way to church, a sudden breeze descended caus-ing his hat to blow off his head and fall into the mud. As he

reached for it, he slipped. He began to curse, shouting and rais-
ing his fist to heaven. 'God damn you. Why do you hate me so
much? Why do you do this to me? You have never done anything
to show you loved me. I God damn hate you! You love everyone
but me. Why? What have I done to you?'

He then heard someone behind him. In his embarrassment,
he realized it was the parish priest. The man began to apologize
and suggest he really hadn't meant everything he'd said. But the
wise old priest said, 'It's all right son. That is probably the first
honest prayer you ever said?'

Developing a sense of spirituality requires a faith in something or someone you cannot see. For adult children who grew
up in homes in which pain was the central organizing principal,
faith is difficult to achieve. Sometimes faith comes harder to
those who once believed in a greater power than to those who
never had any beliefs. I have found it imperative that we teach
our young people about those concepts which kept Anishinabe
people in harmony prior to contact with the dominant culture.
These teachings have meaning today and are useful to both
Anishinabe and non-Anishinabe people.

The Process of Creating Our Own Spirituality

Through Acceptance We Learn Humility

By recognizing a God or a Creator, we are recognizing that there
is a power greater than ourselves. It requires much humility to
give up a life of self-sufficiency and to seek help from a power
greater than yourself. When we were created, the Great Spirit
breathed into us a little spark of life which is of Him. The Great
Spirit is in all of us. What this means is that I can humbly go to
any of my brothers and sisters, elders, or medicine people and
ask for help without fear of being thought weak or immoral.

We need to understand those things we ultimately have no
control over. When we carefully review any list of things we can
and cannot control, honest assessment will reveal that most
things *are* beyond our control. We cannot control other people.

In fact, all we can control is our own behaviour and our own reactions. We can choose to go to a movie, but we can't control when it starts, who else attends, or what it costs. What we *can* control is the attitude that will determine if we enjoy ourselves. Accepting our limitations as human beings is the first step towards accepting a power greater than ourselves.

When we come to accept that we are creations of the Great Spirit or God, we will know the meaning of 'all our relations.' We will understand that we are one creation of many, including those things we can see and those things we can't see. Creation is the Eastern doorway from which we enter into this world at birth and the Western doorway from which we exit this world in death.

Since all life is based on a circle, and a circle has no beginning and no end, life cannot end in death but rather takes on a different form and meaning. When we understand 'all our relations,' we will know our ancestors are just as much a part of us today as when they were physically walking Mother Earth. In this sense, we are never alone. Our relations are still present to help us.

In this vein, spirituality ensures we will never die but will always have life, much like the Judeo-Christian ethic of rebirth to eternal life. Spirituality is what happens to a father when he sees his daughter being born. It is about that immateriality. In the book *Creation Spirituality*, Matthew Fox talks about the spirit of life being Ruah, breath, wind. He states that to be spiritual is to be filled deeply with Ruah. Those who choose this path must be willing to let go and learn. As Anishinabe people, the Red Road is our path.

On this path, you must walk slowly observing all that is around you. The object of life is not to get to the end of the Red Road but to *enjoy* the journey. That is the fundamental principal of life and of recovery that restored my life.

By Overcoming Fear, We Learn Bravery

For many suffering from alcoholism, asking for help is like

admitting inadequacy. As a tradeoff, they try to 'take care of business' themselves. This tradeoff is reflective of the deep shame inside of us acting like a gigantic hole in our spirits that we can never fill. It is not just an Anishinabe phenomenon but one that is universal.

I cannot imagine living in the fear I did when I was using alcohol and drugs. I thought if people really knew me they would see how weak and vulnerable I felt inside. I tried desperately to present a different image to the world, a false image of security, bravery and a laissez-faire attitude. To all appearances, the world saw a young man who was not afraid to take on the biggest person in the bar regardless of how badly he got beaten. I thought it was better to be beaten and stand up to someone than to turn scared and run.

But it was a false bravery – the alcohol was what made me valiant. The real truth was that I was afraid to face the real issue, dealing with myself and the way that I felt. By running away, I had become my greatest enemy.

Someone once told me courage is not the absence of fear but the overcoming of fear. To be a warrior is to overcome your own fear for the benefit of others. Thus, in sobriety I try to overcome my greatest fears, which are my own feelings. I know I will experience pain and joy, but I now see my feelings as my allies. They tell me when something is good or not so good. They tell me when something is wrong. All I need to do is pay attention to them and not run from them or try to numb the pain with alcohol or drugs. For over seventeen years now, I have relied on this greater power to remain in recovery.

During the loss of my mother, I allowed myself to experience those feelings associated with grief. I cried, took care of my older sister, spoke like an older brother, and helped my father through the difficult time. During this time period, I chose to rely on people who could give me support and encouragement, an elder, my wife, and some close friends. But over the years, I have learned that if we rely on people who rely on addictions, we usually fall with them.

To come to a point of recovery, required a great amount of

bravery. It required facing many of my fears, especially around trusting people. I chose to trust those who are trustworthy. It required me to look at myself instead of blaming others for my problems. It meant taking responsibility for my actions and being honest with everyone around me. I learned that recovery requires great courage, for it is easier to remain sick and in trouble than to claw your way back to a life based on the principals of our ancestors.

When I was in a relationship with an American girl, we would often go to her parents' place. We eventually moved in together, and although her parents tried to be kind to me, my alcoholism was becoming evident to them. They tried to talk their daughter into leaving me, and I saw them as a threat. One day in a drunken stupor I went to their home and screamed obscenities at them. Now, this woman's mother had actually done nothing to me, but in my alcoholic mind I thought she was out to get me. Often alcoholics feel this way – and I was no exception.

Shortly after finding sobriety, I moved back to Fort Frances. One day about two years later I was walking through the mall in International Falls, Minnesota, and I saw an elderly woman I knew well selling tickets at the far end. A feeling of fear and shame swept over my body. Instead of being brave and going up to her and making amends, I headed back to Canada as quickly as possible.

Later that night while attending a self-help meeting, I began to reflect on the experience. It occurred to me that I had acted exactly the same as when I was drunk. I let fear and shame dictate my life instead of my spirituality. I knew that as long as this was left unresolved I was not free to walk down the streets of International Falls. I knew this lady couldn't beat me up or yell louder than I, but for some reason when I saw her I was filled with fear. I knew I had to face my own feelings. I eventually made those amends, and I am now free to walk down any street free of fear.

What I am trying to say is that courage is not about physical strength; it is about being able to confront life and not running away from what we fear.

By Confronting Denial, We Learn to Be Honest

Denial is a defence mechanism allowing us to avoid dealing with the reality of our situation. It tells us the situation is not that bad or that it doesn't exist at all. Its sole purpose is to protect us from any real or imagined pain.

There are four basic ways that people use to protect themselves. They are all or nothing thinking, control, repression, and denial. All or nothing thinking is a symptom of the family's pain because it exemplifies the family's inability to provide the child with predictable perceptions and feelings. All or nothing thinking allows the child to make sense out of senseless situations. In response to the inconsistent family behaviour and outlandish behaviour of parents, children grow up with strict views of right and wrong. In the child's mind, the parents are good, which means the child is bad. This kind of thinking carries with it a great sense of shame, loss, abandonment, and grief because it is better for a child to believe herself 'bad' than to deal with the belief that the parent is 'bad.' Having a caretaker who is 'bad' would create fear and insecurity.

Control is another method we use to defend ourselves from the pain of our childhood. As children we grow up feeling powerless to change things yet responsible for the things that have happened. As we grow up, we attempt to gain control over our lives and others' to compensate for the lack of control we had as children. To be out of control would be a reminder of our out of control alcoholic parent. Being out of control symbolizes weakness, vulnerability, and dependency. As adults, we avoid these feelings by attempting to control situations and other people.

People who are controllers are easy to identity. They operate from the premise that their way is the right way. They usually do not allow others to make the decisions or take the appropriate actions.

My need for control after recovery was tremendous. To feel safe in my sobriety, I had to be in charge. I was always afraid to fly in an aircraft, and had thought it was because I had heard many stories about plane crashes; however, one day I was forced to fly from Fort Frances to Toronto. I flew on a small aircraft to Thunder Bay and there transferred to a larger DC–9. As we taxied down the runway, I felt a wave of panic rush through my body. How could I trust my life to a machine and pilots I did not even know? The more I thought about it, the more panic I felt. By the time we were airborne, I was nearly hyperventilating. Suddenly I heard the captain talking in a calm voice. He was welcoming us aboard the aircraft and telling us how high we were going to fly as well as our speed and expected time of arrival in Toronto. Just knowing this information made me feel a little better about my flight.

When my wife and I were first married, I tried my best to control her because I didn't trust her completely. It wasn't anything she did. Instead it was a reflection of my own sense of inadequacy. I thought anyone could steal her away from me. After working on my own self-esteem and learning to love myself, the desire to control her left me.

Repression can be described as pushing our feelings deep inside of us. I used repression as a means of denying my feelings for most of my life. Looking back, I believe I repressed my feeling mainly because I was afraid to express them and felt no one would support or validate my feelings. Whatever the reason, my need to express feelings were usually met whenever I drank alcohol. Alcohol lowered my inhibitions and created a false sense of bravery. The end result was that whenever I drank I usually ended up fighting or crying. When I was drunk, it wasn't unusual for me to sit up until four o'clock in the morning listening to country and western songs in 'crying jags.'

Other times I would fight the biggest guy in the bar. Although I only weighed 130 pounds, the rage, anger, and alcohol replaced my usual common sense. Madness may be a better word to describe antagonizing a man twice my size to the point where he would lose control. Unfortunately, the reality was that these men were usually just as drunk as I and therefore did not have much self-control either.

In recovery our biggest challenge is that of honesty. Denial and honesty can not coexist at the same moment. Honesty means we are aware of ourselves and how we impact on the world around us. Very often alcoholics find the most difficult part of dealing with denial is the effect their drinking has on those they love. They sometimes believe when they are drinking they only hurt themselves. Many abusive men believe they are the victims and are forced to hurt their partners because their partners will not obey or comply with all their wishes. In this way, they deny their responsibility for their own actions. The first step towards honesty is talking about the realities. Alcoholics need to talk about their alcoholism and wife abusers need to talk about their abusive behaviour.

In Anishinabe teachings, we encourage all of our people to talk freely among each other. But after generations of being told when to speak, as in school, we feel discouraged from doing so. As a person in recovery, I must allow others to recover, and therefore it is my responsibility to be nonjudgmental and to allow others their disclosures.

When I learned to hunt, my father taught me to speak in different ways using sign language and gestures to communicate. Although in certain situations we learned to be silent, we allowed ourselves to communicate on other levels. Body language was a way in which Anishinabe people spoke to each other. Silence did not mean that people kept secrets. In contemporary teachings, lack of verbal communication is considered part of the illness; however, we know that people are always communicating whether they are speaking or not. We need to be able to listen on other levels. In recovery, we should always watch what our bodies are telling us. Unlike our mind, our bodies never lie to us.

After I had become more open about my abuse, someone made the remark that they couldn't believe I had been sexually abused. I remember becoming upset with their reaction because I assumed they did not believe me. What they were telling me was that I had come a long way from the lost, angry adolescent they once knew. By being honest and confronting this person, my body was agreeing with what I was saying, unlike years ago when I would say everything was fine as I stumbled from bar to bar.

As an alcoholic, even when everyone walked out on me and I began to feel suicidal, I still refused to accept the idea that I was alcoholic. Everything in me fought against the idea I could not drink safely or control the amount of alcohol I drank. Instead, I lived in a world built on the illusion that things would be different next time. All I had to do was change drinks, change the people I drank with, change the time of day I drank, change everything except me. In my denial and delusion, I ran from city to city and from relationship to relationship, never once stopping to wonder why my problems continued to follow me. If I had, I might have realized why I couldn't run away.

Recovery meant learning the truth about myself and loving myself in spite of that truth. It took a great deal of courage to say I was a victim of sexual abuse, an alcoholic, an adult child of an alcoholic, a victim of childhood poverty, a victim of racism, and a drug addict. It took even greater courage to take that frightened child inside of me and lead it out of the dark forest of denial to face the tears and pain associated with recovery.

Although recovery was difficult and many times I wanted to quit, go back to the bottle and forget, my warrior spirit kept me going. I did not give in to easy relapse, but took the hardest step in my recovery – reaching out to someone else. By doing so, I learned there are many just like me. In my self-help meetings, and later in healing circles, I found solace in belonging to a group. Looking back over those times when I wanted to die, I realized all I really wanted was a friend. I found that in recovery.

Through Our Ignorance, We Learn Wisdom

Having lived in a world of delusion and denial, I did not understand what it meant to make good choices. I had thought that young people were supposed to make mistakes and do crazy and sometimes ridiculous things. Looking back on my life, I realized I never learned from my mistakes, but instead made them over and over again. Some of this can be attributed to delusion; some can be attributed to ignorance. The delusion entered in when I believed everything was all right, that I was all right. Ignorance came into play when I thought these things that had happened to me were normal.

The cycle of violence and alcoholism kept me in a constant state of delusion and ignorance. It wasn't until I left treatment that I began to develop some wisdom. One of the wisest things I learned was that I had to learn not only from my mistakes but from the mistakes of others. I am grateful to be able to say that in all these years I have not relapsed into active alcoholism. While attending self-help meetings, I would listen to people talk about their experience with relapse and how this relapse had helped them develop a newfound appreciation for sobriety. I began to think that perhaps I should relapse to gain this appreciation – until a young man showed up at a meeting and announced that one of our members had relapsed.

While in his relapse, this person had died in a car accident in which he also killed a young mother and her child. Hearing this, I felt a strong sense of gratitude. I was grateful because it did not happen to me. I remembered a slogan, 'But for the grace of God, there go I.' Right then and there, I knew I might only get one chance of recovery and that if I relapsed there was no guarantee I would make it back. Real wisdom comes when we can learn from the experience of others. In other words, you don't have to make all of the mistakes yourself.

Since recovery, I have spent a fair amount of time studying to become a social worker and addictions counsellor. Knowledge itself does not make one wise; it is the way in which the knowledge is used. Some of the wisest and most brilliant healers I have met have been people with little or no formal mainstream training or education. They have been educated and trained in a different way. What these people had was a natural ability to listen to another person. Wisdom comes from our ability to not just hear what a person is saying but to listen carefully to what he is saying. Many of our elders do not have PhDs; nevertheless, years of living in harmony with Mother Earth have given them a great gift. Experience is one of our greatest teachers.

From Our Selfishness Comes an Ability to Share

We cannot live our lives in isolation and expect to be happy and connected to others. Those growing up in homes organized around pain are not always skilled in sharing themselves with others. Since there is usually very little balance in their families, they either self-disclose and trust everyone or are secretive and trust no one. Finding balance in terms of what we disclose or share with others should under all circumstances be an exclusive goal.

Trust takes time to develop, and sharing oneself with another person should be considered a sacred and special experience. Above all, the sharing of oneself should be the choice of the one doing the sharing. Recovery is about choice making and being responsible for the choices we make. Choosing to share oneself with another should take place without coercion. I remember attending my first self-help meeting which dealt with family of origin issues. The people there were very trusting and I wanted to be like them.

As I continued to attend meetings, I began to disclose a little at a time and eventually was able to disclose even my darkest secrets. Maybe part of that is because as I recovered from my childhood trauma shame was not the enemy it once was. After a while, I did not care who learned about my sexual abuse or my alcoholism. Finally I had accepted my life in its totality and its reality. I neither feared nor was ashamed of it. I did not want these things to happen, but they did.

As I began to trust in myself, I began to see that although others could hurt me, I was the one who held the key to how I reacted to the hurt. I could choose to keep the hurt inside me or talk it out with a counsellor, friend, or whomever I trusted. Whomever I chose to confide in, I was the one empowered to deal with the hurt. Pain was no longer an opportunity to mistrust but an opportunity to discover trust.

By Overcoming Our Shame, We Learn to Love Ourselves

I was ashamed to be an Indian. I hated watching movies where Indians were portrayed as savages. Someone once told me that shame was the feeling of emptiness which tells us no matter what we do, it will never be good enough.

I spent the first part of my life proving to myself I was inadequate. Alcohol for a brief moment in time changed that. It made me confident, witty, intellectual, everything I really wanted to be. I wasn't afraid. In time, people began to see me as a drunk and they began to avoid me. I felt even worse about myself. I sought out people who were just as sick as me, or if not worse. I started drinking with those people who drank on the streets, all the while feeling superior to them.

But while in treatment, I was given some tools that would help me stay clean and sober. I began to use the most important tool the Creator gave me, which was my mouth. I began to talk about how I felt growing up. Surprisingly, people listened and understood me. I talked about the shame I felt as a young Anishinabe in a school that did not understand me. I began to get in touch with the wounded child inside and I began to tell his story. The shame I felt inside began to dissipate. I began to see myself in a different light, a light more forgiving and accepting of my human imperfections.

Recently I was asked to do a workshop on self-esteem. What I talked about was shame and how to rid ourselves of the shame by talking about it. We can develop great theories about self-esteem, but nothing will change unless we begin to disclose the real hurt inside us. By talking about those hurts, we feel them, get angry or sad, find understanding, and release them. This processing of shame brings about a different perspective. We may see ourselves as people with something to give the world instead of people wanting something from it.

The transformations that must take place in recovery are transformations of the spirit. Without gaining a spiritual sense of ourselves, we cannot complete the circle of recovery.

We Learn to Love Ourselves and Care about Others

'I don't care' was one of the slogans I relied on to avoid feeling hurt or angry. I often used it to pretend nothing bothered me. It was my way of trying to demonstrate to others that I was in control. What I was really doing was protecting myself. Love is unconditional. It asks only to be respected and appreciated. When I indulged in alcohol and drugs, I didn't care about myself. To recover I had to recapture my spirit so I could begin to care about myself and others.

Someone once told me that love was unselfish. I had to begin by loving myself to be able to love others. In my experience, loving myself was the most difficult part of the recovery process simply because my inner child felt himself to be deeply unlovable. In my feeling of not being good enough to love, I needed to protect myself, so I developed an attitude of noncommitment and noncaring. However, deep within was a strong desire to love and to be loved. In spite of outward appearances, I secretly wished someone would love me. The problem was that in spite of how much love or kindness someone showed me it would never be enough .

Deep inside, I felt I was flawed, inadequate, and unlovable. I thought everyone could see right through me and would quickly see that I was not worthy of being loved. I thought that the best I could manage would be to put up with myself. The idea of loving myself seemed beyond my comprehension. Self-loathing came much more easily than self-love.

Since I did not love myself, I did not have the capacity to love others the way they deserved to be loved. I chose people who had problems with intimacy and closeness similar to my own. In this way, I subconsciously never had to deal with the fear of being vulnerable. I could live in a world where no one knew me and I knew no one. Risking intimacy was too great a danger, and one from which I ran.

Throughout my recovery, I began to know and respect myself. I began to search for those things I felt were missing in my life. When spirituality began to fill the void inside, I became ready to form an intimate relationship with another person, a relationship which was based on love instead of sex.

The creation of healthy relationships takes time to develop. The elders of our culture explain that relationships are like pearls which need time and patience to reach their real beauty. I have noticed that relationships pass through stages (as shown in the Relationship Medicine Wheel, Figure 7) and that often people do not allow themselves to advance to the next stage.

The first stage of relationship takes place when people are simply acquaintances,. We have many acquaintances, and many of our relationships never move past this stage. Moving beyond means a deeper commitment to develop and maintain the relationship. Sometimes people keep relationships at this stage because they are afraid of letting others know them.

The next stage in relationship development is the companionship stage, where the people involved begin to do things together on a regular basis. They may frequently go for coffee, enjoy conversation, or they may go to dances. At this stage in the relationship, deeper commitment is being developed. It isn't until the next stage, one in which friendship develops, that people begin to feel deeply committed to each other.

For healthy relationships to develop, we need to pass through these stages before we get to the fourth and final stage of a relationship, the stage of the lover.

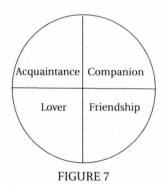

FIGURE 7

Choosing to be lovers requires the greatest degree of commitment of the stages. It means being intimate or sharing oneself on all four levels of human existence: physical, mental, emotional, and spiritual. I believe people get into trouble with their relationships for a number of reasons. One, they carry around baggage from the past, including not taking responsibility for themselves by rationalizing, and two, they do not allow themselves time to move through four stages of relationship development.

One of the problems associated with growing up in a home organized around pain is we never really get a clear understanding of relationship development. Instead of learning how to develop healthy relationships, we learn the art of developing *unhealthy* relationships by moving from acquaintance to companion to lover. To have healthy relationships, our partners must also be our friends.

One of the things about friendship is that we respect our friends' boundaries and their rights to choose to live their lives in accordance with their values and beliefs. We do not control or use power as a binding force. Instead we use similar interests and recognize our partner may have other friends and interests outside of us. This means we must trust, our partners in the relationship. Without trust, we are already alone, and the relationship becomes unsatisfying.

One important thing to remember is that if both partners are willing they can go back through the stages of relationship development to become friends by sharing with and respecting each other, thereby improving their intimate time together. Of course, this intimacy does not always mean sexual intercourse. We carry on social and intellectual intercourse with people all the time.

Regardless of where we are in our relationships, it is our beliefs, values, and teachings about relationships that will determine the kinds of relationships we have in our lives. Anishinabe beliefs are that relationships are the key factors in healing. They are the core of our spirituality. It is not the way in which we pray but the relationship between ourselves and the Creator that is paramount. This belief permeates all our relations.

Without the recognition of spirituality, our relationships are superficial at best. By going through the four stages of relationship development, we stand a better chance of survival. This means that the relationships we have with those we love will be based on a level of spirituality. Even our sexual relations can then be considered spiritual. We will feel closer to our partner and more bonded to those who are important to us.

If we don't pass through these stages, we often do not really get to know the person we are involved with. Eventually we become disillusioned and frustrated. I often describe this as the little boy who keeps looking for something in relationships that he can not find in himself. Our need for fulfilment compels us from one relationship to the next. It becomes a drive that never ends. We end up wondering what is wrong with them or what is wrong with us.

Until we begin to work through some of these issues, we will never have the relationships we desire. By developing and integrating the concepts listed in this chapter, we can start to fill the voids of loneliness and emptiness we feel. By becoming our own best friend and loving ourselves enough to develop a sense of spirituality, we can feel the connection that we want with our partner, our children, and our friends. We can become open and honest about ourselves, seeking neither to hide nor be defensive, because we know we can always trust and count on our ownselves.

By Giving Up Power-Control, We Learn Equality

The final concept helping us to develop our spirituality and facilitate healing is the bringing of equality into all our relationships. It is important to see the good in everyone, to see how everyone within this circle we call life is important and necessary. If this were not so, the Creator would not have created it so.

Our children can be our greatest teachers and our strongest support system. Many times after a hard and frustrating day at the office I have asked my daughter, Nakita-Rose, for a hug. I usually say, 'Daddy needs a hug.' After spending some time with her, things do not seem as difficult or frustrating as they were.

Seeing my daughter as an equal does not mean I let her do whatever she wants. What it means is that I can draw strength from her and she from me. We can share love and understanding instead of my being afraid to nurture or be nurtured by her. Sometimes she will comb my hair and put nice bows in it. She is telling me that she loves me.

Our wives and partners are our equals and were created to stand beside us, not ahead or behind us. My wife and I share many things. We hunt together, play golf, baseball, cook, clean, and share child care. I do not see myself as being above those duties. As equals, I believe we share greater intimacy than we could if one of us were dominant. I believe by being equals we are in the true sense partners, both capable of making adult decisions.

Within inequality in relationships lies the potential for one partner to become victim or aggressor. Instead of working through problems, issues become a matter of power and control. Even communication becomes an issue of who wins the war of words, with no resolutions by consensus. The mainstream legal and economic system is based on who wins. The one with the best lawyer or most money eventually is recognized in this world as the winner.

In the spirit world, the real winners are those who help others and see all creation as equal. The true test of humanity is to help those still struggling to find recovery and to make recovery available to those still suffering the ravages of poverty, addictions, racism, and other social injustices. To be equal, we do not all have to have the same material possessions. What we need is entitlement to the opportunity to grow towards our fullest potential. By practising sharing in relationships, we can create solid relationships based on equality. When equality exists, abuse cannot.